The Ingenious Mr Avison

Making Music and Money

in Eighteenth-Century Newcastle

ALL Gentlemen and Ladies that are willing to Encourage a Subscription now on Foot, for a Concert of Vocal and Instrumental MUSICK, to be held at the Assembly-Room, are desir'd to send in their Names to Messiures Brown and Sanderson, Watch-makers at the Head of the Side, where on Payment of 5 s. one Half of the Subscription, they will receive a Ticket for the Season, which will admit two Ladies, or one Gentleman. It is also desir'd that those who have subscribed, and live in the Country, wou'd order any Person in Town to receive their Tickets, which will be deliver'd on Payment of the above-mentioned Sum.———NB. The first Concert will be perform'd on the 2d of October, being the first Thursday after Michaelmas-day, and will continue every other Thursday till the Lady-day ensuing.

For his first concert, advertised in 1735, Charles Avison was canny enough to offer tickets for one gentleman, or two ladies, for half a guinea (as no lady would ever attend on her own).

The Ingenious Mr Avison

Making Music and Money

in Eighteenth-Century Newcastle

Roz Southey, Margaret Maddison, David Hughes

Avison Ensemble

~

Tyne Bridge Publishing

Acknowledgements

Front cover: *The Sharp Family* by Johann Zoffany, oil on canvas, 1779-1781, by courtesy of the National Portrait Gallery, London and the Lloyd Baker Trustees. The remarkable Sharp family gave concerts in London as an orchestra from the 1750s.

Back cover, half-title page, and page 3 of colour section: *Charles Avison* by Francis Lindo, 1761, courtesy of St Nicholas' Cathedral, Newcastle.

Unless otherwise indicated illustrations are from the collections of Newcastle Libraries.

Tyne Bridge Publishing thank the Literary and Philosophical Society, Newcastle; Tyne and Wear Museums; St Nicholas' Cathedral, Newcastle; the National Portrait Gallery, London; Lloyd Baker Trustees; the Foundling Museum, London.

The Avison Ensemble thank their funding partners: Arts Council North East; Esmée Fairbairn Foundation; Friends of the Avison Ensemble; Hedley Denton Trust; Heritage Lottery Fund; International Music & Art Foundation; Newcastle City Council; Northern Rock Foundation; Rothley Trust; The Monument Trust; The Shears Foundation. The Avison Live project forms part of NewcastleGateshead's world-class programme of events in 2009, managed by Culture[10].

©Roz Southey, Margaret Maddison, David Hughes, 2009

Published by
City of Newcastle upon Tyne
Newcastle Libraries
Tyne Bridge Publishing
In association with the Avison Ensemble
2009

Tyne Bridge Publishing
Newcastle Libraries
PO Box 88
Newcastle upon Tyne
NE99 1DX

www.tynebridgepublishing.co.uk   www.avisonensemble.com

ISBN: 978 1857951295

British Library Cataloguing in Publication data: a catalogue record for this book is available from the British Library.

Printed by Elanders Hindson, North Tyneside

Contents

Isaac Thompson's map of Newcastle upon Tyne, 1746. The town was still largely enclosed within its walls and was reached from the south by its one medieval bridge.

Who was Charles Avison?

Charles Avison is one of those figures of history whose name is better known than his life. His music has recently enjoyed a revival after suffering a great deal of neglect since his death in 1770, but relatively little has been written about him. A number of articles about him have appeared in academic journals; they contain much interesting information as well as some misdirection although a recent study of 18th-century music in the North East has attempted to put him in his historical and social context.[1] None of this, however, is available to the general reader and music-lover; he is mentioned rarely in books on North East history, usually meriting only a paragraph or two even where he does appear.

The Avison Ensemble, a nationally – and internationally – known group that aims to perform Charles Avison's music in as authentic a manner as possible, has decided that the time is ripe for a more detailed study. February 2009 marks the 300th anniversary of Charles Avison's baptism and it seems appropriate to mark the occasion with the first full biography of the composer.

If Charles Avison had been merely one of the lesser composers of 18th century England, it would be hard to justify a such a lengthy study – but Avison lived in interesting times. In medieval days and up to the English Civil War in the mid-17th century, musicians worked under a system of patronage; they were employed by and composed for the court, nobility, the church, and occasionally other bodies such as guilds and town councils. But the civil war broke down this system; the financial burden of the war left the court and aristocracy impoverished and unable to support cultural activities in the way it had

Charles Avison

previously; ecclesiastical employers such as cathedrals took a long time to recover from the depredations of Oliver Cromwell's supporters, who had dismantled their organs and disbanded their choirs. Musicians were forced to find new ways to earn a living, and over the next century there developed a new commercialisation of music (and other leisure activities) which saw, for the first time, the rise of what we now call 'the audience'. This new system, based on concerts and other entertainments which were open to anyone who could afford to pay the price of admission, opened up music to a much wider section of the population and encouraged new inventions (the clarinet, for instance), new styles and new ways of thinking about music.

But there were disadvantages to the commercial system. If audiences were to continue to attend musical entertainments, they had to be given what they wanted – an idea that rapidly led to an excess of showiness and virtuosity, to banal reliance on novelties and fashion, to a plethora of child prodigies who could be counted upon to engage the sympathies of the audience, and to the composition of ephemeral 'occasional' pieces such as the popular 'battle' piece, featuring musical depictions of gunshots, cannon fire and the groans of the dying. Serious music-lovers deplored almost all these tendencies but no musician wanting to make a living could afford to ignore them.

Charles Avison's significance is that he was one of a new breed of musicians who managed to conduct a very successful business life, combining the best of the old and new systems, without ever compromising his musical principles. In writing, he deplored the breakdown of the old patronage system, but in practice he coped very well with commercial pressures, exhibiting a canny financial good sense and ending his life a rich man. In some ways, he was a very modern figure, understanding promotion and marketing in ways that we would recognise today. But he also produced compositions that adhered firmly to his belief that the best music was simple and heartfelt, and which appealed to a wide range of people throughout the country; the style of his musical writing allowed a wide range of musical amateurs to enjoy playing his works.

That is not to say that his professional life was trouble free. He occasionally misjudged his audience, giving rise to controversy, and throughout his life he was wary of opposition, and suspicious of anyone who seemed to threaten his position – perhaps a natural reaction in days where illness or a change in fashion could mean poverty was only a short step away. A certain insecurity sometimes shows through. Towards the end of his life, too, he was clearly aware that he was becoming old-fashioned in many ways, that the style of music he preferred was being overtaken by new styles and new fashions.

It is difficult to judge a man's character from the fragments of evidence that remain, but Avison seems to have been a man of charm and energy; he had remarkably little difficulty in the early years of his career in making friends with influential and wealthy members of the local gentry. He read a great deal, probably spoke or at least understood several foreign languages, enjoyed discussions on politics, literature and ideas with good friends, was clearly a man of tact and diplomacy in dealing with his social superiors, and was never short of good ideas for his concerts. He was patriotic and generous, and his family life – apart from the usual tragedies caused by the high infant mortality of the time – seems to have been happy.

If his music looked back to earlier times (increasingly so as his life wore on) his thinking was free-ranging and *avant-garde*. His discussions with the gentlemen who supported him gave rise to a book – *An Essay on Musical Expression* – which was the first book in English to deal with the philosophical aspects of music that were exercising minds in continental Europe. The book raised a furore; Avison, never one to shirk an argument, entered into the controversy energetically.

Avison's position at the beginning of the commercialisation of music, and his contribution to the development of ideas on music, make him an important figure in the history of music. Moreover, there is a new appreciation of his music particularly when played on period instruments by groups like the Avison Ensemble. For all these reasons, a biography seems long overdue. In writing it, we have assumed no musical knowledge on the part of the reader; the general music-lover will enjoy placing Avison into his historical setting, and the lover of history will gain new enlightenment on the history of the North East by a glimpse of its cultural life, an aspect of history often neglected. Those looking for detailed analysis of Avison's music will find it elsewhere; our concern has been to explain the music by putting it, and its composer, into their social and historical context; to show a man who was acutely of his times, caught between admiration of the old system and old music, yet dealing capably with the new commercialisation and new ideas, and adding greatly to discussions of them.

~

Money in the 18th century was pre-decimal: 12 pence made one shilling, 20 shillings made one pound. One guinea was 21 shillings. An average wage for a labourer was around one shilling per day; town organists in the North East generally earned around £20-£25 a year. The headmaster of Newcastle Grammar School was paid £125 per annum although, being a clergyman, he had a number of additional sources of income.

Until 1752, the year began on March 25; the months of January and February, and the first part of March, were considered to belong to what we would consider to be the previous year. This can cause, and indeed has caused, considerable confusion, particularly in the early part of Avison's life. We have here converted all such dates to the modern equivalent.

A new life

'1708/9: 16 February [baptised] Charles to Richd Avison Musician Nolt Market'
Register of St John's Church, Newcastle

St John's church in Newcastle upon Tyne is a small medieval building with a squat tower that, in the 18th century, shadowed an extensive churchyard. Sitting in the middle of Westgate Street, next to large gardens, it was in the more genteel part of town, and had an active and wealthy congregation.[2] A fine new peal of six bells had been hung in 1706, and in 1709 there were plans to rebuild the porch and to install a gallery round the inside of the church, so that more worshippers could be accommodated.[3]

As far as musicians in the town were concerned, the church was of little interest for it had no organ and therefore no salaried organist's post. The only music was provided by the congregation, singing metrical psalms led by the parish clerk and his pitchpipe. On February 16, 1709, however, the church was the centre of attention for musician Richard Avison and his wife, Ann, as they arrived for the baptism of their seventh child.

Richard and Ann were not native to Newcastle. They had come to the town in the middle of 1702, most likely from Yorkshire, where the surname Avison, or Aveson, was widespread at the time. They

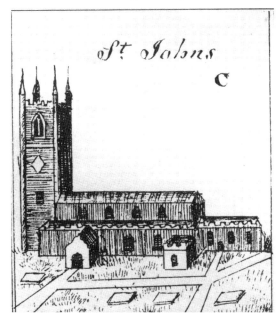

St John's Church, from Corbridge's map of 1723.

brought with them at least two young sons and came so that Richard could take up a new job – that of wait, or town musician.

Newcastle must have promised profitable new opportunities for the couple. The 17th and 18th centuries were good times to be living in an urban environment; towns and cities were growing in size and importance, and rapidly absorbing immigrants from the countryside. They provided markets for agricultural produce and a range of financial and legal services that were much in demand from the local gentry. Newcastle had the extra advantage of being a port, trading with the Baltic and Europe; the shipping facilities were used by a wide range of industries – the coal trade, soap making, glass manufacture, potteries and engraving. In 1700 Newcastle was the fourth largest town in England with a population of 18,000 – a size exceeded only by London, Bristol and Norwich.

When the Avisons arrived in 1702, they must have been surprised both by the prosperity of the town and by its appearance; despite its growing prosperity Newcastle retained many of its medieval features. It was small (only 180 acres) and enclosed almost entirely by the town wall that ran for two miles, pierced by six gates and with 17 towers. The wall had once been the strongest in England but was falling into disrepair and becoming inconvenient. In addition, the Lort Burn ran through the centre of the town from north to south, cutting it in two; vehicles could only cross the burn on the riverside or, to the north, outside the town walls at Barras Bridge. Pedestrians were also able to use two footbridges within the walls, the Low and High Bridges.

At the heart of the town was the Quayside, where goods were loaded and unloaded, and the keelmen strutted in their yellow waistcoats. The only bridge across the Tyne was the medieval bridge, lined with houses and shops; towers stood at either end and in the middle – the tower at the Newcastle end was used as a prison. Just off the bridge on the Newcastle side was the impressive, if idiosyncratic, Guildhall, accommodating the fishmarket and overlooking the Sandhill, crowded with shops and coffee houses.

The streets of the lower town were always plagued by smoke from house fires and from small businesses. From the Sandhill and the Quay, only Side and Pilgrim Street, both narrow and winding, tackled the steep slopes to the upper town, a stiff climb for horses and wagons. Pedestrians usually made use of the many stairs that gave access to the streets above. Here were the spaces where the markets were held: the Groat, Flesh, and Bigg (Barley) Markets, all in the

A view of Newcastle in 1745, by Nathaniel Buck. St Nicholas' church dominates.

shadow of the gilded spires of St Nicholas' church.

Beyond that were the upper reaches of Pilgrim Street and Westgate Street, residential streets where the wealthier people lived, overshadowed by the medieval gates, and the towers and spires of the town's four churches. Under the tall square keep of the looming castle and the Black Gate, which gave access into the castle precincts, crowded the tenements of the poor.

But it was not all coal dust and narrow lanes, shrieking markets and stinking fish. The town enclosed many green spaces. The better houses had gardens; former monastery sites – Blackfriars, Whitefriars, and Greyfriars – were now open spaces in private or Corporation ownership. To the west of the town was the Forth, a field where fairs were held; outside the town walls on

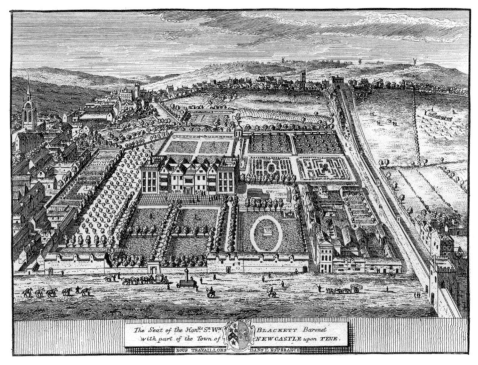

The sumptuous residence of the Blackett family, the Newe House on Pilgrim Street, Newcastle, in 1702.

this side were gardens with summerhouses and the Forth House, which had carefully laid-out walks around a bowling green approached by an avenue of trees.

Leisure was an increasing priority in English towns and cities. When the local gentry came into the towns to consult their lawyers, to attend the Assizes or to do business, they wanted entertainments to occupy their evenings. Their wives and families took the opportunity to renew acquaintance with old friends or with relatives, and looked for ways to beguile the long days. Theatre companies had visited Newcastle since at least the 16th century; other entertainments included horse racing, cock fighting, bull baiting and prize fighting. For those who preferred more sedate activities, there were assemblies – both for dancing and for cards – and walks around the town walls, even visits to see the dissected bodies at the Barber Surgeons' Hall. Many wanted musical entertainments, at home or in public, or to learn how to play an instrument

A view of St Nicholas' Church in 1715, by W. Horsley.

themselves. There were potentially plenty of opportunities for a good musician and teacher to exploit.

The family that came to St John's church on February 16, 1709, had been extended since Richard and Ann came to Newcastle, but fate had not always been kind. Ann had given birth to a third son in November 1703 although the parish clerk at St John's had neglected to note the child's name in the register. (This was probably Edward.) Then the couple suffered a series of tragedies. Their first daughter, Elisabeth, was baptised in February 1705, and another son, Richard, in May 1706 but both died in October 1706 within four days of each other; perhaps they were both victims of some childhood illness, like measles or scarlet fever. Ann became pregnant again very quickly, and another son, John, was born in August 1707. However, he lived only a few days.

With this recent history, there must have been some considerable anxiety in Richard and Ann's minds as to whether their latest child would survive. In St

John's church on that February day, he was baptised in the name of Charles and went home to his three older surviving brothers – William, Edward and Thomas. Whatever the anxiety at the time of his birth, he did survive, and thrived, and was to become better-known that anyone could have suspected.

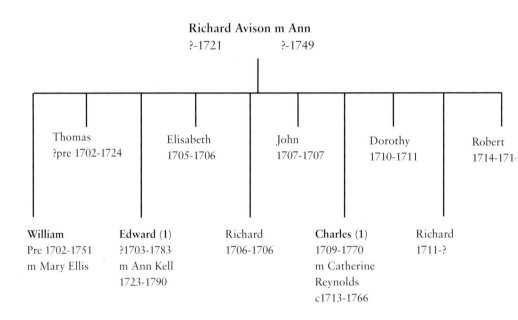

Friends and Neighbours

'A good company of Musick'
Minutes of Common Council of Newcastle Corporation, October 8, 1795

Charles was not the last of Richard's and Ann's children but he was almost certainly the last to survive. When he was a year and a half old, his mother gave birth to another daughter, Dorothy, who died after only nine months. Two more boys, Richard and Robert, followed in 1711 and 1714; Robert died at only a month old – of Richard nothing more can be traced.

Avison therefore grew up in a household of boys: William was probably the oldest, around ten years older than Charles, then came Thomas and Edward. Charles was the youngest by six years. The family seems to have been moderately well-off and lived in a house near the Nolt Market, a cattle market at the bottom of Newgate Street; their home was opposite the Nungate, a lane leading to the large open field called the Nuns. No doubt the boys played there as children. By 1714, however, the family had moved to Westgate.

Richard described himself in parish registers as a wait, one of the musicians employed by Newcastle Town Corporation to accompany civic processions and ceremonial occasions.[4] The pay was low – only £5 per annum for each of the town's five waits – but the post allowed the waits to take in paying pupils, and they were also employed by the town guilds to provide music at their feasts. In addition, they were available for private hire. Thomas Kirk, a Yorkshireman visiting the area in 1677 on his way north to Scotland, recounted how he and friends hired the Newcastle waits ('the wind-music and the fiddles of the town') to accompany them downriver to North Shields and Tynemouth. As they came home again, the heavens opened and poured rain on them; the gentlemen, however, insisted that the musicians continue to play even though they were 'almost drowned'.

Richard Avison was not in the town for that expedition but he would almost certainly have taken part in an evening of entertainment organised in

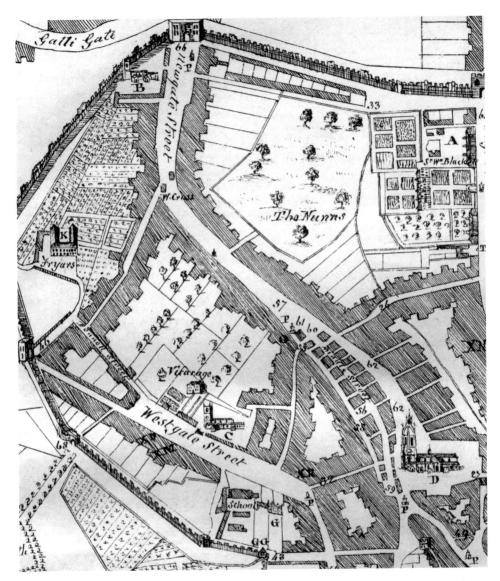

The north-west corner of Newcastle's town walls in 1723. This detail from Corbridge's map of 1723 shows the area around Avison's birthplace and the three churches which would be important to him: St John's (C), St Andrew's (B), and St Nicholas' (D). The Assembly House, which would also become very important to Avison, is marked XD and is opposite St John's on Westgate Street.

Newcastle Guildhall, the centre of local government, in 1786.

August 1705 by three young gentlemen who were friends of a Mr Green in the Bigg Market. The gentleman had supper and dancing with 'all the most pretty goddesses of the town'; the ladies grew tired and went home, but the gentlemen were not ready for sleep. The waits were sent for. Two oboes and two violins appeared and the party marched round the town from three till six in the morning, serenading the ladies, who appeared at their windows to receive the compliment.[5]

The waits as a body would have been impressive, dressed in livery or uniform; no description of the Newcastle livery survives but in York the waits had scarlet coats with buttons and trimmings, and silver lace on their hats.[6] Newcastle Corporation allowed £5 every year to buy new cloaks for the waits which suggests that they were dressed equally splendidly.

Unfortunately, their performance did not live up to their appearance. The low wage may have attracted a poor quality of applicant or encouraged financial abuses. In 1705, only three years after the Avisons' arrival in the town, the Corporation realised that one of the waits, Robert Blenkinsop, was blind and too infirm to perform (although he does not seem to have been particularly old and survived at least another 20 years). The Corporation brought forward another man, John Jubb, to 'make them a better company and a good concert of music';[7] Blenkinsop was given an annual pension of £2 10s a year and guaranteed another £7 per annum to be paid to him by the other waits, including Richard, out of their own salaries.

The Avison family were plainly on good terms with Jubb and other members of the waits including Robert Martin (whose two sons were also later to be waits) and Henry Kell, who was a carpenter by trade. Jubb was clearly not as effective as the Corporation had hoped, however; two years after Avison's birth, in 1711, complaints were made of 'irregular practices ... to the great prejudice of the company of waits'.[8] Robert Martin was named as one of the chief culprits and an enquiry ordered into the whole business, but nothing ever seems to have come of it and Robert remained a wait until his death in the 1730s.

There is no evidence that Richard Avison was involved in anything untoward, although the accusations must have caused anxiety in the household; if he had been dismissed, the finances of the family would have been severely strained. He had his teaching, of course, always the mainstay of any musician's income, which probably brought a stream of people to the house daily, and he also had another salaried post – that of organist at St Mary's church in Gateshead. This brought in a further £8 every year.[9]

Organists were always amongst the best paid of musicians and organists' posts were much sought after. Newcastle had four churches but only two, St Nicholas' and All Saints, possessed organs. St Nicholas' was the more prestigious, paying £25 per annum in 1700 with an additional honorarium of £5; in the early 1720s the salary was increased to £40 a year, and extra money could be earned for tuning the organ. All Saints was less well paid but the annual salary of £16 was still well worth having.[10]

When Richard and Ann first came to Newcastle, the organist at St Nicholas' was Samuel Nicholls, about whom almost nothing is known except that his brother, John, was reprimanded in 1710 for illegally letting some of the pews in the organ loft. Nicholls was succeeded in 1719, when Avison was ten, by Thomas Powell who had the reputation of being a good teacher.

Debt and poverty were threats hanging constantly over the heads of any

St Mary's, Gateshead, around 1825. Richard Avison was organist here.

family in the early 18th century; illness or unemployment, even on a temporary basis, could quickly reduce a family to destitution. For musicians, disaster could strike appallingly swiftly for any number of reasons: illness or injury could prevent a musician playing his instrument, a change in musical fashions or a new attractive competitor might tempt customers and patrons away. Penury was never far off; this was a lesson that Avison seems to have learned early and determined to avoid – his later career was to show him to be not only an excellent musician but also a highly competent businessman.

In the early years of his life, Avison must have had plenty of examples to teach him what to avoid. Thomas Powell of St Nicholas' died in debt; Robert Blenkinsop, the wait who was too ill to play, struggled throughout his later years to persuade his fellow waits to pay him the pension the Corporation had ordered. And, at All Saints, perhaps the most colourful character in Newcastle's musical life of the time was constantly struggling to make ends meet.

Avison was five years old when the Corporation appointed a new organist to All Saints; it is unlikely that the Corporation knew their new appointee's full history. 'Mr Francis de Prendecourt' they called him, and promised him £16 per annum providing he trained up one of the boys from the charity school to be his deputy. For François Prendcourt, who occasionally styled himself Captain Prendcourt, All Saints was a new low after a life spent in much more prominent circles. In the mid-1680s, he had travelled from France to be one of the musicians at the court of the new, Catholic, king of England, James II; barely had he arrived in the country, however, than James's Protestant subjects rose up and forced him to flee. Most of James's musicians chose exile with him, but Prendcourt lingered in England, apparently travelling about the country and, very possibly, acting as a spy for his former master.[11]

All Saints church around 1723, from Corbridge's map.

In 1705, Prendcourt was in Derby; he may have been in Kendal (well-known for its large community of Catholics) in 1710. By 1714, he was reduced to applying for the post of organist at All Saints; this was an act of desperation for he had once sworn that he would never play in, or compose for, a Protestant church. However, needs must: Prendcourt was to remain at All Saints for the next 11 years, sinking deeper and deeper into debt and repeatedly applying to the Corporation for charitable payments, before he died in September 1725.

~

In addition to all these local musicians, the Avison family probably saw, from time to time, some more famous performers. Durham Cathedral was only a couple of hours' travel away on horseback and the Dean and Chapter there had a policy of scouring the country for the best organists and singers. Two years after Avison's birth, they brought north as organist 19-year-old Londoner, James Hesletine, a man of fiery and uncertain temper with whom Charles was to clash a number of times in the middle of the century.

Hesletine's salary of £70 per annum must have seemed almost unimaginable to the Avison family.[12]

From time to time, famous musicians passed through Newcastle while travelling between London and Edinburgh, both cities with active musical lives. These musicians were not averse to stopping for a week or two, perhaps putting on a concert to defray travelling costs, or playing in someone else's entertainment. This habit was one of which Charles took advantage on several occasions in later years.

In addition to the musical families of the area, the Avisons would also have been in contact with a wide range of the social spectrum, with rich tradespeople and with gentry families, many of whom may have been Richard Avison's pupils or who may have employed him to teach their children. Little information remains to suggest who these men may have been but one was certainly the merchant and gentleman, Ralph Jenison, who may have proved extremely beneficial to Avison in his teenage years.

Childhood

'1721 29 November: Richard Avison one of the Newcastle Waits; dyed here'
Registers of St Oswald's church, Durham

Avison's childhood is shrouded in mystery – only fragments of information suggest what may have happened. In later life, he was an educated man but there is no record of him attending Newcastle's Grammar School so perhaps he and his brothers went instead to the charity school attached to St John's Church. The school was only a little older than Charles himself, having been set up in 1705 by John Ord of Fenham, to teach 44 boys. The Ord family were later to be influential in Avison's career in other ways.

As far as musical training was concerned, Richard in all likelihood undertook this himself. Nothing is known of Thomas but the other three brothers seem all to have been musical. Edward, however, chose not to pursue music professionally; in 1716, when Avison was only seven years old, Edward took up an apprenticeship with a Newcastle tailor, John Hudson. Richard and Ann spent £10 on the apprenticeship. Richard was recorded on documents as 'gentleman', a term generally applied to someone living on unearned income. Clearly the family was well-off.[13]

William, probably the oldest brother, was clearly destined for a musical career and in 1720, at the age of 18, applied for the job of organist at Holy Trinity, Hull, reputedly England's richest parish church. As was usual, William had to contest the post with the other applicant, a Mr Barlow.[14] Elections for organists' jobs usually consisted of the candidates playing before an audience of churchwardens, clerics and vestrymen; a later candidate for the Holy Trinity job had not only to play the organ but also to put on a concert as the organist was the principal promoter of local concerts and had to prove his suitability for this role. William won a resounding victory, receiving 31 votes out of a possible 33; his reward was a salary of £30 per annum, which he would certainly have augmented by taking on pupils.

With Edward and William both in employment elsewhere, Avison found himself in a greatly reduced household. Thought must have been given to his own future; would he, like William, pursue a musical career, or should he take up an apprenticeship in another trade, like Edward? There is no

Holy Trinity, Hull.

clear indication of Ann and Richard's plans for their youngest surviving son but in any case, everything was thrown into confusion the year following William's move to Hull, for in November 1721, Richard suddenly died.

Richard was probably still in early middle-age, perhaps in his late forties or early fifties. In late 1721, he went on a visit to Durham, possibly to teach a pupil or to visit friends, and died there; he was buried in St Oswald's churchyard on November 29. In Newcastle, Ann was left a widow with at least one son, possibly two, still at home. Avison was 12 years old.

How the family coped, emotionally and financially, with Richard's loss, is not known. One of Ann's first acts was to visit the churchwardens of St Mary's church in Gateshead to collect Richard's last half year's salary.[15] William no doubt supported his mother and brothers, and it is possible that Thomas too may have had a job. Young Charles must have been expected to contribute to the household. It has been suggested that he was apprenticed to local merchant and MP for Northumberland, Ralph Jenison, of whom he later spoke fondly in the dedication of one of his compositions, saying that not only had he had 'the early good fortune of [Jenison's] Approbation' but also that the compositions were 'the Fruits of those vacant hours, I was favour'd with in Your Service'.[16] There is no evidence of this apprenticeship, however, and it seems highly unlikely that Charles Avison would have been apprenticed to anyone as important as Jenison; such an apprenticeship would have been sought after by many leading families. Guild documents and Admission books (recording the admission of Newcastle freemen) survive for the appropriate dates and do not record any data for Charles Avison although they do record details of his brother Edward's career.[17] Nor does Jenison's name appear. In addition, if Charles Avison was apprenticed to Jenison, it is hard to see why he would have given up so potentially lucrative a career for the much more insecure profession of musician.

The significant words in the dedication of Opus 1 are 'in your service'; it is possible that these words, which generally are used in connection with servants, signify that Avison was in Jenison's household either as a household musician, or perhaps as a talented youngster who was nominally a servant but taken in to be given training with any later success reflecting glory on his master and patron. In 1733, Edward advertised for a violin that had gone astray after being sent to Jenison's house at Walworth; the violin was probably intended for Avison and lends credence to the idea that he was in Jenison's household at that period. In the absence of firm evidence, however, all this must be speculation.

Three years after Richard's death, in 1724, the family was depleted further when Avison's brother Thomas died. Two years after that, Ann became a grandmother and Avison an uncle when William's first son was born in Hull. But the child was illegitimate, the result of a liaison between William and Elizabeth Carver, daughter of the Holy Trinity sexton; the child was named for his father, but there does not seem to have been any suggestion that William and Elizabeth should marry, and Avison and his mother may never have seen the child.

Charles Avison's teenage years are almost a blank but he clearly continued to play and to study music, and may have intended to pursue a musical career from the start. In the early 1730s, therefore, when he was a little over 20 years old, he took the logical next step for any musician with ambition – he left the area for London.

London!

'Many Courts, many Men, many Customs'
Newcastle Courant September 17, 1768

London had always been the centre of music-making in England.[18] Its royal court employed a large number of musicians, as did its nobles; St Paul's Cathedral and Westminster Abbey offered opportunities for singers and organists. The civil war in the mid-17th century had, however, done untold damage, not merely politically but also culturally. Oliver Cromwell's adherents had disbanded cathedral choirs throughout the country, and torn out organs in protest against what they saw as over-elaborate worship. Theatres had been closed and public music-making severely curtailed. The King's Band and the Chapel of the Royal Household, which provided the court with secular and sacred music respectively, were both cut to almost nothing. Worse, the cost of the war and the struggles associated with it left the monarchy and nobility in several financial straits, so that even when Charles II regained his throne in 1660, he was not able to restore the old glories of the court.

He did try, however. Within days of returning in triumph to the capital, he appointed over 40 musicians to provide him with the latest music. Unfortunately, he never had enough money to pay them.

Deep in debt, relying on theatre performances and on teaching to make ends meet, London's musicians, headed by the leader of the King's Band, John Bannister, came up with a new and unique form of entertainment – the public concert. Under the old system, only the aristocracy and their hangers-on heard the latest music; in the new entertainment, anyone could listen, providing they had a shilling to pay an entrance fee at the door. The idea opened up the audience for music, shifting the emphasis from the relatively small social elite of the aristocracy towards the burgeoning middle-classes who were thriving on trade, and marks the start of a new commercialisation of music and a new consumerism. For musicians who were willing to embrace the new trend and possessed a strong streak of entrepreneurial ability, it could be extremely

Mr JOHN BANNISTER.

John Bannister, inventor of the public concert, reproduced from John Hawkins',
General History of the Science and Practice of Music, 1776.

profitable. Avison was later to exploit it very effectively.

Concerts were a huge success from the very beginning. The first concert with a paying audience was held by Bannister in London in 1672 and the idea was rapidly taken up by a number of other people who put on both individual concerts and series. The idea spread from London to the regions, to Bath and Oxford and then into Scotland, to Edinburgh. Concerts became part of the social round. In London, there was the Italian opera too, and the English ballad operas that satirised them. Music and musical entertainments began to enjoy a huge popularity.

All this offered potentially extremely lucrative opportunities for musicians and many a musician in the English regions was tempted to take advantage. Unfortunately, in this high-powered musical world, the Italian was king, and Italian opera, Italian singers and Italian violinists were idolised; even an average foreign performer had a better chance of success in the capital than a good English player. Some Englishmen tried to trick the system by changing their names in order to attract some of the glamour of the foreign although the disguises were often very thin; John Hebden of York, for instance, masqueraded in at least one concert as Signor Hebdeni.[19]

Despite the challenges, there were always people who thought they could succeed spectacularly in London. Richard Elford, one of the singing men at Durham Cathedral, persuaded the Dean and Chapter to finance a trip to the capital in 1699, ostensibly to improve his singing. The Dean and Chapter clearly expected him to study hard with various singing teachers and return with improved musicianship, but as soon as he reached London, Elford, clearly stage struck, headed straight for the theatres. He ignored commands to return home and was promptly dismissed. Unluckily, London audiences admired his singing but not his acting, which was evidently wooden. Eventually he found two jobs, in the choirs of St Paul's Cathedral and of Westminster Abbey, and seems to have been much lauded. On the whole, he probably did not regret his audacious adventure.[20]

Charles Avison probably did not have the dewy-eyed optimism of Elford although no doubt he would have embraced acclaim had it come. His aim in

Durham in the 18th century.

going to London was more practical. He was following in the footsteps of many another musician in the North East and going to the capital for training and study, for what was often known as 'improvement'. The Dean and Chapter's unfortunate experiences with Elford did not deter them from sponsoring other singing men on trips to London, sometimes for short periods of only a month or two, sometimes for a year or more. A trip to the capital was a sign that a musician was taking his profession seriously and could be a good selling point on returning home; a newspaper advertisement stressing experience in London often appealed to the snobbishness of regional audiences.

The trip was, of course, expensive and it is not known who helped Avison with his expenses, he may have travelled south with Jenison, and at Jenison's expense, when the MP went south for the Parliamentary sessions – Avison probably travelled to the heartland of the new commercialism under the auspices of a patron, representative of the old system. Once in London, he could earn his own keep by teaching and by playing in various performances. No one knows, either, exactly when he travelled south, although it was certainly in the first few years of the 1730s, when Avison was in his early twenties and probably in late 1733.[21] He was certainly in London in March 1734.

Many rumours abound as to the exact nature of Avison's activities at this point, including claims that he travelled as far as Italy. This was stated with some certainty by Charles Burney in his *General History of Music* published in 1776; Burney, however, was relying on second-hand information.[22] Certainly in later years Avison talked of performances of his music in Paris and Milan which are hard to explain unless he had contacts there, and in the 1750s he commented on the continental style of psalm-singing in terms that suggest he himself had heard it.[23] Some of the rumours, however, may have been sparked off by the fact that in London Avison was lucky enough to be able to study with one of the most famous and admired Italian composers and performers of the period, Francesco Geminiani.

Geminiani was in his late forties when Avison met him. A native of Lucca, Geminiani had travelled throughout Italy in his youth, studying both with the famed Corelli and with Alessandro Scarlatti before coming to London in 1714. For 20 years he had been lauded in his adopted country, praised as a virtuoso violinist (although he rarely gave public performances) and applauded as one of the best composers of the time. Ironically, just at the moment Avison went to London to study with him, his popularity was beginning to slip into a permanent decline.[24]

Avison, however, never ceased to admire him. In later life he paid a poignant and unstinting tribute to his teacher in a letter written to the *Newcastle Courant* in September 1768. Geminiani, he said, 'spoke all the European languages, and his conversation was lively

Francesco Geminiani, from Hawkins' General History of the Science and Practice of Music, 1776.

and entertaining … He had seen many Courts, many Men, many Customs … He loved the Arts, and assisted many Artists.' This cosmopolitan man, according to Avison, loved music, painting and sculpture and advised his pupil not to accept praise if he knew it to be undeserved, nor to get down-hearted if his merits were neglected. Above all, he recommended truth and simplicity as being of paramount importance, in music and in life.[25]

Under Geminiani's guidance, Avison probably made his first adult attempts at composition. A cantata, *Delia and Thyrsis*, seems to have been composed in London and refers in its words to 'my virgin muse', suggesting that this is a very early work. It may have received its first performance on March 20, 1734, when Avison held his only known concert in the capital – a benefit concert from which he would take all the profits.[26]

Concert promotion could be a highly profitable business, as many a musician had found since the first concerts in 1672, but the scope for disaster was also great. A well-known or fashionable musician would have no difficulty in pulling in a large audience and thereby make a substantial profit; a young unknown, particularly an Englishman in London, faced great difficulties in drumming up interest. Avison would probably have had to make personal visits to the music-going ladies and gentlemen to try and sell his tickets, a procedure which he later followed in Newcastle. He faced other difficulties too. In the capital it was impossible to choose a day on which there were no competing entertainments, the cost of hiring a room and heating and lighting it would be expensive, and he would have to hire other musicians to play in his concert band.

Avison was therefore taking a big risk in putting on a concert, although Geminiani's support may have been useful; the venue, Hickford's Rooms, was where Geminiani had himself promoted a series of concerts two years previously. Unsurprisingly, the music played, according to his advertisement, consisted of works by Geminiani and the Italian's own teacher, Corelli, together with songs by Handel. The advertisement also promised solos on the flute, violin and harpsichord, and Avison may have played all these himself; almost every musician of the period was expected to play several instruments to a high standard. Unluckily, no review of the concert survives, and it is not known whether it was a success or not.

There was one other musician in London with whom Avison might have become friendly, and who may even have provided the songs at his concert. Thomas Mountier, who had started his career as a chorister at Chichester Cathedral, was one of the lucky English musicians who managed to become well-known in London; for a few years he was much admired in concerts there. The two men were to find themselves unexpectedly collaborating on a new venture – not in London, but back in Avison's native North East.

A new Entertainment

'A Subscription now on Foot, for a Concert of Vocal and Instrumental Musick'
Newcastle Courant September 20, 1735

Thomas Mountier left London in early 1735 and in April was appointed a singing man at Durham Cathedral at £50 per annum, a high salary for that period. Within two months of his arrival in the North East, he put on a concert in Newcastle, followed a month later by another in Durham; the fact that he chose to appear first in Newcastle may have had something to do with the size of the town but it is tempting to think that he may have been influenced by his friendship with Avison.[27]

Avison's return home probably took place at much the same time and, like Mountier, he would have been looking for a salaried post. This was always the ambition of any musician; a salaried post gave personal finances a secure footing and could then be supplemented by activities such as teaching where income could be much more variable. Such posts, particularly the well-paid ones, were few and far between. There were rumours even in his own day that in 1735 Avison was offered the job of organist at York Minster at this time; he was only 25 years old but many a musician had taken a similar post at an even earlier age. This may have been just a rumour; no evidence survives at York to confirm or disprove the offer. If Avison was offered the job, however, he turned it down and with it the chance of earning £40 a year.

Perhaps he simply wanted to go home. His mother was still alive and he may have wanted to make her life easier by supporting her from his earnings. His patrons and potential patrons too – the Ords and Jenisons amongst them – were in Newcastle and he must have hoped for help from them; starting in a new place would not have been easy, although his brother William was managing well in Hull. His other surviving brother, Edward, had completed his apprenticeship and, after an argument caused by his master's unpaid debts, had been made a Freeman of the town.[28] Edward set up as a staymaker, with a shop on the steep winding Side, then moved to the Fleshmarket next to the Black

Bull and Post Boy Inn; he lived in a house on High Bridge.

Perhaps Avison had been forewarned of a vacancy for an organist in Newcastle. In early October 1734, the parishioners of the parish of St John's had decided that they wanted to install an organ in the church where Avison had been baptised. There was widespread support for the project and a great deal of money was raised; in a letter to the town Corporation, they said that 'they had at their own expense found, provided and set up an organ ... which cost them a considerable amount of money'. Knowing that the Corporation paid the salaries of the organists at St Nicholas' and All Saints, they thought they should pay for the St John's organist too; the Corporation agreed to pay a salary of £20 a year.

The job seems to have been already Avison's. When the Corporation agreed to pay the salary in October 1735 he was named as having been already appointed, although the organ was not quite ready to play. There is no record of him having to go through an election as had his brother William – perhaps his local connections,

St John's church around 1790.

and the presence of some of his patrons on the Corporation, had got him the job.

Before the organ was playable and Avison took up his post (probably around Christmas 1735), another opportunity came his way. At the time, it must have seemed merely another source of income but over the next 35 years it, and Avison, became a Newcastle institution. Twelve gentlemen decided to set up a winter series of concerts.

In the first third of the century, the North East had only occasionally enjoyed the entertainment that was so fashionable in London, Bath and Edinburgh. The first known concert in the region took place in 1712 although there may have been earlier concerts that have gone unrecorded.[29] The 1712 concert took place in Mr Harris's dancing school on Westgate Road and offered 'Instrumental Musick; as Opera-Tunes, Italian-Solio's, Sonata's, Overtures, &c. upon the following Instruments, viz. Spinett, Trumpet, Hautboy, Violins, Bass-Viols, Bassoons, &c'.[30] Since that year, there had only been isolated concerts put on both by local

The Grammar School on Westgate Street.

musicians and by visitors to the area. In 1725, for instance, a man who described himself as 'a famous Lute-Master' put on a concert at the Grammar School on Westgate Street offering as star attraction his nine-year-old daughter who sang Italian and English songs.[31] The concert, like many others, seems to have been in the nature of an advertisement to tempt local ladies and gentlemen to take lessons with him.

No more concerts are recorded until the end of 1733 when there seems to have been a sudden upsurge in interest. On October 8, 'a Sett of the finest and best Masters from York, Durham &c.' put on a concert at the Grammar School and on December 6, 'the best Masters in these Parts' staged another at Mrs Benson's Assembly Room (probably also on Westgate Street). They were upstaged, however, by two visitors to the area, Nathaniel and Charles Love (possibly father and son) who visited the region briefly in mid-November, putting on concerts in Sunderland and Newcastle. Mrs Benson's Assembly Room was the venue for the Newcastle concert too and the two men played solos (mainly from Handel's operas) on the trumpet, French-horn, oboe and flute. Mr Love senior also played a Cuckoo solo and a Quaker's sermon on the violin.[32]

Music-lovers were rather more sparsely done by in 1734 as only one record of a concert survives but the chief performer, Claudius Heron, was a link to another of Avison's wealthy supporters. Heron was, despite his name, a Frenchman, in the employ of George Bowes of Gibside; in the early 1730s, he acted as a kind of factotum to Bowes, accompanying his master on his travels, paying the expenses of the trips, organising lodgings and meals, the cleaning of clothes and the purchasing of gunpowder, and travelling abroad on errands. He was also an excellent cellist, playing a concerto and several solos on the instrument at the Grammar School on June 12. In later years, Heron and Avison were to become well-acquainted, and Bowes and his second wife were to become Avison's patrons.[33] Avison was already beginning to understand the new commercial system well but nonetheless he still cultivated the old style of patron, and some, like Bowes, were to support him and employ him for many years. Although the new system was rapidly advancing, there was no clear-cut break with the old ways.

These concerts, and Mountier's in June and July 1735, may well have convinced a number of local gentlemen that there was a considerable local audience for concerts and that a winter series might be financially viable. It is more than possible that Avison, with his recent experience of London entertainments, suggested the idea to them, exploiting a certain snobbishness which may have attracted them to something that was so popular in the capital. In late September 1735, an advertisement was placed in the *Newcastle Courant* inviting anyone interested to send in their names: 'All Gentlemen and Ladies that are willing to encourage a Subscription now on Foot, for a Concert of Vocal and Instrumental MUSICK, to be held at the Assembly-Room, are desir'd to send in their Names to Messiures Brown and Sanderson, Watch-makers at the head of the Side.'[34] A subscription ticket cost ten shillings and admitted one Gentleman or two Ladies (on the principle that no lady would

ALL Gentlemen and Ladies that are willing to Encourage a Subscription now on Foot, for a Concert of Vocal and Instrumental MUSICK, to be held at the Assembly-Room, are desir'd to send in their Names to Messiures Brown and Sanderson, Watch-makers at the Head of the Side, where on Payment of 5 s. one Half of the Subscription, they will receive a Ticket for the Season, which will admit two Ladies, or one Gentleman. It is also desir'd that those who have subscribed, and live in the Country, wou'd order any Person in Town to receive their Tickets, which will be deliver'd on Payment of the above-mentioned Sum. ——NB. The first Concert will be perform'd on the 2d of October, being the first Thursday after Michaelmas-day, and will continue every other Thursday till the Lady-day ensuing.

attend unaccompanied). The first concert was fixed for October 2 and there
was to be another every fortnight until early February; each concert would last
three hours, including the interval. As soon as the advertisement was published,
someone pointed out that the date for the first concert clashed with Sunderland
Races, so the concert was brought forward a day to October 1.

After the initial advertisement, the newspapers are silent about the series
until April 1736, when a violent dispute suddenly broke out. For weeks, the
Courant was full of vitriolic letters – extraordinarily long missives penned in
white-hot anger by various of the gentlemen involved in the series. Accusations
were made of 'scurrilous language and opprobius Names', of 'ill-nature' and
'captious Humours'. All had clearly not been well.[35]

The problem seems to have lain in the organisation of the series. The 12
gentlemen who proposed the concerts had originally intended to choose the
music, plan the programmes and direct rehearsals, in order that no one
performer should be given greater prominence than another. But in practice,
the gentlemen had either been weak, or lazy, or perhaps just too busy and the
performers had been left to get on with it. The result was a clash between two
strong personalities.

At the centre of the quarrel were a Swiss violinist, whose name has not
survived, but who led the band, and a man who was referred to throughout the
correspondence merely as 'a modest young man'. This name seems to have
originally coined as a sarcastic insult by the supporters of the Swiss violinist
but was then taken up as a compliment by their opponents. The 'modest young
man' appears to have been Avison.

Who started the dispute is impossible to say. The Swiss (often referred to
sarcastically by his opponents as 'the nimble-finger'd Swiss') was clearly an
excellent violinist, much admired by audiences. The applause he received may
have gone to his head, although to be fair this accusation comes from the pen
of his opponents: 'The nimble-finger'd Swiss, upon his Receiving every Night
an extravagant Demand for his Dexterity [imagined] himself a Person of much
Consequence.' It is plain from the accounts of his playing, however, that he was
not a man to whom Geminiani's plea for simplicity meant very much, which
must have irritated Avison.

The violinist's supporters claimed that he was annoyed because he felt that
'the modest young man' was taking too much on himself as regards the day-to-
day organisation of the concerts. Worse, the 'modest young man' – Avison –

was, they claimed, trying to undermine the Swiss's position. Avison had in his possession all the music and instruments belonging to the subscription concert; the Swiss and his friends claimed that he had refused to let them borrow the books for practice purposes. They also said that he frequently changed the pieces for the concert after the lunchtime rehearsal, sometimes as little as two hours before the concert.

Avison's supporters rushed to his defence, dismissing their opponents' arguments as 'specious'. They said that the music books were always available, then got down to some subtle insults. Why, they asked innocently, should the Swiss want to borrow the books? Surely a professional musician should not need to practice? Surely he ought to be able to sight-read the music in which case last-minute changes should not disconcert him. Hints were dropped that the Swiss's real motive was something rather more sordid; the whole affair, Avison's supporters said, simply came down to a pay dispute. The Swiss was paid 10 shillings for each performance but wanted 15 – derided as 'London' wages.

After several vicious letters exchanged in the column of the *Courant* by the two parties of supporters, the Swiss threatened to withdraw from the concerts unless his demands were met, calculating that the concerts could not continue without him. The gentlemen organising the concerts, however, called his bluff. No more money was forthcoming and the Swiss withdrew in affronted dignity.

The concert series did not collapse. A new leader of the band was found – Avison's 12 year old apprentice (possibly a boy called George Williams). The move caused a storm of fury on the Swiss's side, being clearly meant to suggest that the job was easy enough for a child to do. After many insults and arguments, a proposal was put forward by Avison's supporters to settle the dispute. They suggested a musical duel.

The 'duel', surprisingly, was not to take place between the Swiss and Avison, but between the Swiss and Avison's 12-year-old apprentice. The two agreed to meet at Mrs Hill's tavern in the Fleshmarket on Thursday May 20, 1736; each was to take an accompanist and some music. Each competitor was to play his own music then to swap with his opponent and play his opponent's music by sight.

There was much arguing over who should judge the competition. Thomas Powell, organist of St Nicholas, was suggested but he was considered to be too close a friend of the Swiss. Thomas Mountier was then proposed but he was judged too close a friend of Avison. Finally, both sides accepted that James Hesletine of Durham Cathedral was sufficiently impartial.

Hesletine probably had not the slightest knowledge of the 'duel'. When the Swiss arrived for the contest it was to find that his opponent was absent and instead he faced a number of gentlemen who put a new set of conditions to him. He chose to retire in injured dignity, sending a note to the *Courant* to blame his opponents for the situation. 'We shall give ourselves no further trouble in answering their reiterated Equivocations, let them write as many Absurdities as they please.'[36]

The Swiss was dignified in retreat; his opponents, Avison's supporters, were exultant and vicious in victory. They sent two mock obituaries to the *Courant*. The first was relatively mild: 'Whereas the nimble-finger'd Swiss, having departed this life on Thursday night last … This is to give full Authority to all Grave-diggers, &c. where-ever they find him, to bury him without any further Ceremony.'[37]

The second obituary was brutal in its ponderous humour, starting: 'We thought it would not be amiss to give a more satisfactory and circumstantial Account of the Death of a little lean cholerick Fidler.' After a long and solemn account of an illness from which the Swiss was supposed to have suffered, the anonymous writer continued:

> 'The Hour of his Death approaching, several Folks drew near to see what sort of an End he would make: He began about half an Hour before he died to rave much, and deliver himself in broken sentences; he had his black Fiddle in his Right Hand, and his Fiddle-Stick in his Left, a Plaister of Crotchets of his own composing defended his Vitals; Thus arm'd, he stood when Time with his Scythe, appear'd for once in the Shape of a young Fidler. The moment his feeble Eyes met his dreadful Antagonist, his Agonies seiz'd him (for you must know that he was always a great enemy to Time), he spit, star'd, stunk, and dy'd.'[38]

This vicious letter, with its snide references to the Swiss's alleged inability to play in time, its inaccuracies (the apprentice did not appear) and its dubious detail (was the Swiss really a left-handed player?) marked the end of the dispute. The Swiss violinist seems to have left Newcastle and is never heard of again. Avison was left in possession of the concerts.

Work and marriage

'It is humbly hoped this Undertaking will meet with some Encouragement'
Newcastle Courant July 29, 1738

Avison's new supremacy in the subscription series was marked by the fact that the only announcement for the second series was tacked onto the end of an advertisement for a concert he held on August 18, 1736. The August concert was for Avison's 'benefit', which meant that all the profits would be his alone. Holding a concert in mid-year, in Race or Assize Week, when the town would be crowded with visitors eager for entertainment, was to become Avison's regular habit and is an early example of his business acumen.

In October 1736, when the subscription series was just beginning again, Avison had other matters on his mind. Another opportunity for professional advancement presented itself unexpectedly; in early October, Thomas Powell, organist of St Nicholas', died.

The position was highly desirable, offering £40 a year, a great advance on the £20 Avison had at St John's and he seems to have had no hesitation in applying for it. Not only was the post the best paid musical job in the town but it had a prestige which came from appointing high-quality musicians; if his application was successful, Avison would have every right to be considered the best musician in Newcastle. This would give him added status, and help to attract pupils. Avison got the job; as with the St John's post, he may have been appointed without an election as no other candidates for the post are known.

Unfortunately, the financial aspects of the appointment were complicated. Powell had died in what the Corporation described as 'poor circumstances' and it was decreed that the money that would have been dedicated to the salary of his successor over the next half year would have to be given to paying off Powell's funeral expenses and his debts. Avison therefore was told that for the first six months of his new post, he would continue to receive only the salary from the St John's job. This meant that there was no money left to pay the new organist at St John's, so an amateur player, James Clark (a saddler by trade) was brought in; he was apparently willing to pay for no salary until the situation at St Nicholas' was regularised.

One of Avison's first acts was to examine the St Nicholas' organ; he rapidly came to the opinion that it was in a bad state and told the Corporation that it was 'so dirty it will be very much damaged if not speedily cleaned'.[39] He may also have brought a new style of church music to the town. An organist was expected to provide two instrumental voluntaries, almost always improvised, during the service, and to accompany the

The Groat Market, looking towards St Nicholas'.

metrical psalms. In the early 18th century there was controversy over the style of music provided by some organists; the *Gentleman's Magazine* reported with some acidity that it was not unknown for snatches of current operatic hits to be incorporated into voluntaries. Avison disapproved of this entirely, writing later that the organist should be extremely cautious of imitating 'common Songs or Airs'; this could only 'too much expose Religion to Contempt and Ridicule'. Music in church, he said, should 'relieve, with religious Chearfulness, the calm and well-disposed heart'.[40]

Avison tried to achieve this desirable end by following Geminiani's precept of simplicity. The only other professional organist in the town apparently did not. Solomon Strolger, a Londoner by birth, had been appointed organist at All Saints when François Prendcourt died in 1725; he received the improved salary of £20 per annum and was at the same time appointed a wait. Strolger's playing may well have been everything Avison disapproved of; many years later, a parishioner described Strolger's playing as 'meaningless rants'.[41]

The 1736-7 season of subscription concerts went almost unnoticed by the local papers even though, in a startling move, the organisers doubled the cost of the subscription. The series probably ran a great deal more smoothly than its predecessor but Avison's attention was elsewhere, on family matters. His financial situation was clearly sound; on June 15, 1736/7, less than two years after his return to the town as just another young musician looking for a job, he had accumulated sufficient income to feel able to marry.

His bride, Catherine Reynolds, is something of a mystery. She was almost certainly not Newcastle-born as her baptism does not appear in any local parish records and may have met Avison in London during his stay there. A family of Reynolds were singers, actors or dancers connected with the Haymarket Theatre; the theatrical connection may explain why she was later derided in print for her lowly birth – actresses were often regarded as little better than prostitutes. No members of Catherine's family are ever mentioned.

The couple made their home in Humble's buildings near the Pullen Market, probably one of the new houses built by John Humble at the west end of High Bridge.[42] In May 1737, Avison's unmarried elder brother Edward advertised that he was moving from the foot of Side to Humble's Buildings and it is likely that their widowed mother, Ann, also joined them there in an extended family group.[43]

Catherine became pregnant very quickly and gave birth to the couple's first child in December 1737. The boy was named Charles for his father and given the usual three godparents: his grandmother, Ann Avison; his uncle, Edward; and a friend of his father's, Nicholas Walton. Godparents were extremely important, as they were expected to take an active interest in the welfare of their godchildren both spiritually and materially. Nicholas Walton of Farnacres in Gateshead was not only a music-lover, but also a wealthy man in the coal trade and may have been one of Avison's early patrons.

Avison's financial situation was good, but the arrival of a child may have strained the family's resources and, in January 1738, Catherine put a notice in

In HUMBLE's Buildings *near the* Pullen-Market,
IS Taught all Kinds of NEEDLE-WORK.
PLAIN-WORK, at 5 s. per Quarter; SHADE-WORK
and EMBROIDERY, at 8 s. per Quarter, and Half a
Crown Entrance, by   CATHERINE AVISON.

Catherine Avison advertises in the Newcastle Courant in January 1738.

the *Newcastle Courant* advertising her services as a teacher of needlework. Catherine taught 'all Kinds of Needlework' including plain work (lessons cost five shillings a quarter) and shade work and embroidery (lessons cost eight shillings a quarter); pupils also paid half a crown entrance when they first started lessons.[44] Whether this continued as a regular source of income is not clear as Catherine did not advertise again; perhaps they were trying to save as much as possible in the early years of their marriage against the inevitable growth of their family and Catherine's teaching may have been abandoned as her husband's income improved.

Meanwhile, the 1737-8 subscription series went ahead as expected and was interrupted only by the death of Queen Caroline which halted all entertainments for a short while. As Avison later explained, however, the concerts were in a rocky state financially.[45]

According to Avison's account (written in 1758) the original series had boasted 170 subscribers, each paying half a guinea; the series, he said, was 'universally encouraged'. The novelty of the enterprise may have appealed to music-lovers and the heat stirred up by the dispute with the Swiss at the end of the series may only have stimulated interest. The 12 organising gentlemen were fired with enthusiasm, and proposed ever bigger ideas, including bringing in more and better performers. A subscription series in York was hiring Italian instrumentalists and singers at the time, and it may be that something of this sort was in the gentlemen's minds.

The doubling of the cost of subscription for the second series had been intended to pay for these ambitious plans but the increase caused the number of subscribers to plummet; Avison later estimated that the number never again exceeded 110. The inevitable result was a large gap between income and expenditure. Given that the majority of the organising gentlemen were wealthy tradesmen, their lack of financial acumen is surprising. Unlike the organisers in York, however, who continued to hire more and more Italians until the series collapsed in bankruptcy, the Newcastle gentlemen took a long cold look at what was happening and decided to do something about it.[46]

Avison may have proffered advice. He certainly indicated his willingness to take on sole responsibility for the series and the gentlemen's appreciation of his abilities is shown by their agreement to give it over into his hands. In July 1738, Avison advertised a concert in Assize Week and attached a paragraph concerning the next year's subscription series, indicating that the gentlemen had resigned its management to him. 'It is humbly hoped,' he wrote, 'that this Undertaking will meet with some Encouragement.'[47] He hoped to succeed where the experienced gentlemen had failed – an audacious undertaking but one to which he was to prove amply equal.

Reaching out to new audiences

'The general Intercourse of Friends and Acquaintances'
Newcastle Journal November 4-11, 1758

Avison's recipe for success was simple; he went back to the original intentions of the 12 gentlemen, reducing the cost of the subscription to its first level of half a guinea and abandoning the gentlemen's ideas for expansion. Amongst the things he had to deal with were heating and lighting the rooms during the performances, the purchase of musical instruments (which belonged to the series rather than to individuals), the buying of music books, and the maintaining of apprentices. This latter he considered to be as important as the rest, possibly because apprentices would play in the concert band.[48]

He later wrote that he considered the ideal size of a concert band to be 17: six first violins and four seconds, four cellos, two double basses and a harpsichord. Wind instruments should not be used with strings as they were 'so different in their Tone' and went sharp as they warmed up, whereas stringed instruments went flat. Only the bassoon was permissible, if played by an expert, to bolster the bass line.[49]

Avison's band was therefore a string band and not a large one, but even so there would not have been enough professional musicians in Newcastle or the surrounding area to fill up the parts. The five waits would naturally take part, together with Avison and any apprentices; these professional musicians would take principal parts in the band. The other parts would have been taken by pupils of the town musicians. These would be wealthy tradesmen or minor gentry – the so-called gentlemen amateurs; as it was not considered appropriate for gentlemen to allow their names to appear these men remain largely anonymous. The 12 organising gentlemen were certainly amongst them, however, as the advertisement announcing Avison's takeover of the concerts stressed that they would continue to play in the band.

This mix of amateur and professional players could cause problems. Avison later wrote of some of the faults found in amateur players with a plaintive air that suggested he was commenting from personal experience. He accused some harpsichord players of continuing to play during pauses in the music, and advised players not to complain if their part was small as it would give them more leisure to listen to everyone else. He suggested that amateur musicians should leave ornamentation of the melody to the professionals, who knew exactly when to put ornaments in and when to leave them out, and pleaded with players to come in at the right time, a problem which arose through 'miscounting of Rests, or depending upon others; and thus render[ed] the whole Performance ragged and unmeaning'.[50] He also asked performers to take notice of crescendos and diminuendos, and condemned players who played the tune an octave higher than written just so the audience could hear and admire them. In addition, he bemoaned the fact that music was often performed after only one rehearsal and without players ever seeing the full score, which meant they concentrated only on their own part and did not consider how the different parts of the work fitted together.[51]

It was difficult to correct such faults. Avison might be rapidly gaining respect for his abilities as a musician but he would still have been regarded by many gentlemen amateurs as a tradesman. The amateurs were his social superiors and frequently his employers, in that they paid him for lessons and bought subscription tickets. The utmost tact would have been required to manage them and improve their playing without giving offence.

Concerts were informal affairs. Many were held on the upper floors of taverns, such as the Red Lion in the North Bailey in Durham, and the Turk's Head in the Bigg Market in Newcastle.[52] The Long Rooms of these taverns were designed for official dinners, allowing sufficient space for a table down the centre of the room, chairs on either side and room for servants to walk around; this was less than ideal for concerts, but the only alternatives were the Assembly

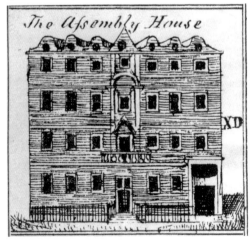

The Assembly House, Westgate Street, around 1723, from Corbridge's map.

Rooms in each town which were intended for dancing and were therefore equally long and thin in order to accommodate sets of dancers. Assembly Rooms often had galleries for musicians but these usually only had room for four or eight players; staging had therefore to be brought in if it was wished to raise the performers

above audience level. Most of the players stood, seats being provided only for the harpsichordist and any cellists. The harpsichord, probably played by Avison in Newcastle concerts, would stand in the centre of the stage and players would stand around it.

The audience would not expect to sit still and listen in silence. Concerts were as much social occasions as musical events and often the motive for attending was to see friends and relations. Indeed, Avison himself gave this as one of the chief justifications for putting on concerts: 'it keeps alive, and improves the social and benevolent Affections, by the general Intercourse of Friends and Acquaintances'.[53] As a result, the audience would not sit in formal rows but would instead have comfortable armchairs, or promenade about the room, conversing. It was considered to be the mark of a good performer if he or she could silence the chatterers.

~

In the hurly-burly of a busy professional life and the changes caused by marriage and a new baby, Avison still found time for leisure activities. Around 1740, he was probably a founder member of the Newcastle Literary Club, a group of about nine young men who met once a week between 6pm and 11pm in the evening. Each man took turns in the Chair and introduced a book from which extracts were read aloud; the book was then discussed and refreshments supplied. Subjects discussed included religion and morality, politics and history, philosophy, the arts, science and poetry, and the club room was decorated with busts of favourite authors. The club also had a philanthropic element – each member paid 18 pence a night for expenses, and part of this was allocated as a fund for the poor. It was, however, a short-lived club as some of the members moved away from the town.[54]

Avison also found time to indulge in his first love as far as music was concerned – composition. As a friend later said: 'Let him have his pen and ink, his candle, his ruled paper and his harpsichord, and he looks no farther, at most no farther than the performance of his music'.[55] The first printed results of this passion for composition were published in 1737 – a set of six trio sonatas, dedicated to his patron, Ralph Jenison; according to Avison's preface, they were composed in quiet moments while in Jenison's service – 'the fruits of those vacant hours' – a description that hardly suggests Avison's work for Jenison was strenuous.[56] The pieces had almost certainly been performed in private before publication, probably in the meetings of the Newcastle Musical Society. Musical societies – private meetings of the gentlemen amateurs – were very popular throughout the 18th century and this is the first hint that there was one in Newcastle; many of its members were probably the gentlemen who had organised the first series of the subscription concerts.[57] These societies usually employed professional musicians to direct their playing and it is likely that the Newcastle Musical Society hired Avison. The gentlemen, says Avison's preface, had liked the trios so much that they urged him to publish the works.

A second publication saw the light of day in 1740 when Avison published a set of six concertos for string orchestra. These had also clearly been written for performance by Newcastle musicians, this time in concerts; this consideration may have influenced the form taken by the music. The *concerto grosso* form was particularly well-suited to bands made up of a mix of amateur and professional players; amateur players could be given relatively simple parts while the professional players took more demanding solos. The concertos in Opus 2 also avoided awkward keys and difficult techniques such as double-stopping which might have caused amateurs to stumble. The concertos were sufficiently popular for a second edition to be published in 1742 with the addition of two new works.

Opus 2 was dedicated to a gentleman whom Avison must have met in London, Colonel John Blathwayt, an enthusiastic amateur musician and patron of several musical bodies in the capital.[58] Blathwayt had plainly helped Avison for the dedication to Opus 2 refers to 'valuable opportunities of improving' which Avison had gained through Blathwayt's 'generous assistance'.

These publications were not commissioned but financed by the subscription method; in effect, the volumes were sold before they were printed by obtaining advance orders. Subscribers then had the satisfaction of seeing their names in print at the beginning of the book. But Avison is unlikely to have considered publication without having a fair certainty that the gentlemen whom he taught and who patronised him would purchase copies; their urgings to publish must have implied a ready market for the works. Thus the old patronage system merged with new commercial practices and the subscription lists in Avison's music over the year chart his friendships and his professional contacts, both in London and in the North East, and indeed throughout the country as more and more musical societies found his music ideally suited to their abilities.

~

Throughout the late 1730s and the early 1740s, Avison's and Catherine's family continued to grow. In January 1740, Catherine gave birth to a daughter named for her mother; a little over a year later in March 1741, a son, Richard, was born. Unhappily, Richard died in January 1742 aged only 10 months but Catherine was already pregnant again and gave birth to another daughter, Ann, in September of the same year. As the second edition of the Opus 2 concertos came off the press, the family that celebrated consisted of a son aged five and two daughters, one aged two years, the other newly born. From Hull, too, came news that Avison's elder brother, William, had married, to a woman called Mary Ellis.

Avison and Catherine continued to enlist the aid of wealthy acquaintances to act as godparents for their children. Baby Catherine, baptised in January 1740, had as godmothers Mrs Jane Walton (probably the wife of Nicholas Walton who was young Charles' godfather) and Mrs Ann Jacques (probably a wealthy widow). The baby's godfather was Anthony Isaacson junior, whose father had held the profitable post of Collector of Customs in the port of Newcastle, and who was related to Edward Montagu and his wife Elizabeth (the famous blue-stocking writer). Isaacson himself was a wealthy coalowner. It is remarkable that Avison, the son of a town musician and a tradesman by profession, should have been able to persuade such wealthy men to act as godparents to his children, and suggests that he was an energetic man of strong and attractive character.

Amongst the gentlemen who befriended him were some who lived further afield. For many years, he maintained a friendship with William Mason, a cleric at York Minster; Mason, the son of the Vicar of Holy Trinity, Hull, may have been introduced to Avison by his brother William. He corresponded with contacts in London and Oxford on various musical topics. In addition, he had extensive contacts in Cumberland. These may have originated when he was asked to perform professionally with the Musical Society at Carlisle; he encountered there Captain John Bernard Gilpin and became an occasional member of Gilpin's circle of gentlemen who met to play music and to discuss painting and philosophy. The group included members of

From the collections of Literary & Philosophical Society, Newcastle

William Mason, Avison's friend, from the frontispiece to his Works, 1811.

Gilpin's family, as well as Leonard Smelt (a military engineer and later friend of George III), the physical and experimental chemist, William Brownrigg, and the Dean of Carlisle Cathedral, Robert Bolton.[59]

But the member of the circle with whom Avison developed the closest friendship was John Brown, canon of Carlisle. Brown was a multifaceted man: he was an excellent violinist, an author on many subjects and a talented amateur painter and he could be amusing company. However, he suffered periods of suicidal depression and could be extremely difficult to deal with.[60] He and Avison were to remain friends for nearly 30 years.

In the early 1740s, therefore, Avison was beginning to become much more well known, both in the North East and outside it, and his financial situation was improving all the time. Even greater success was to follow with the publication, in 1744, of perhaps his most famous compositions, concertos based on works by Domenico Scarlatti.

In the company of patrons

'Paid and given Mr Avison for his trouble'
Accounts of Mary Bowes, December 28, 1745

Ironically, the concertos that have since become Avison's best-known works were not considered worthy of an Opus number at the time – his Opus 3 did not appear until 1751. The 1744 concertos are not original compositions but arrangements of works by Italian composer Domenico Scarlatti. Scarlatti's harpsichord sonatas were enjoying a vogue in England but were difficult to play; Avison clearly had this in mind when he decided to arrange the works for performance with his Newcastle concert band. He pointed out that few performers, and certainly not amateur players, could play Scarlatti's sonatas properly; his aim therefore was to simplify the works and put them in a form that was more accessible.

He had to make considerable changes to fit the keyboard originals for a string band. The source he used had almost exclusively quick movements, so he imported slow movements from other Scarlatti works to make up the usual concerto form, which consisted of two fast and two slow movements. In addition, he did not hesitate to alter the harmonies if he thought them wrong, or to add or omit material where he believed it necessary. Some alterations simplified difficult passages which his amateur players would have found tricky. The success of his efforts can be measured to some degree by the number of musical societies, always made up largely of amateur players, who subscribed to these, and his other, works. Avison's ability to write for the kind of bands that were the bedrock of regional concert series was already sure and effective.

~

Professionally, Avison thrived in the mid- to late-1740s; domestically, he and Catherine suffered a mixture of joy and sorrow, all too familiar to parents of the time when infant mortality was high. In March 1744, Catherine gave birth to another daughter, Jane, who was named after one of her godmothers, Jane Ellison, a well-off single woman living in Durham and a cousin of the Ellisons

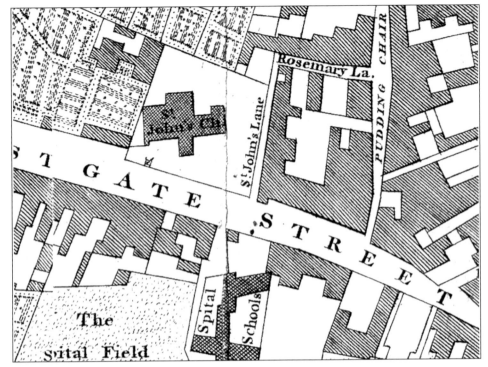

This detail from Charles Hutton's map of 1769 shows where Rosemary Lane was situated, near St John's, off Pudding Chare.

of Gateshead Park.[61] Nine months after Jane's birth, however, in December, young Charles, now seven years old, died.

Between October 1744 and June 1745, the family (now consisting of Avison, Catherine, and three daughters – newly born Jane, Ann aged one and Catherine aged five) moved from Humble's Buildings to Rosemary Lane. This was in an attractive, leafy part of town near St John's Church, and was the home of well-off tradesmen. The house the family occupied was probably on the corner of Pudding Chare and Rosemary Lane, now long since demolished. They took with them an apprentice or two and several servants. It is unlikely that Catherine needed to continue giving sewing lessons. Avison's brother, Edward probably continued to live in Humble's Buildings with their mother, Ann.

In February 1746, two-year-old Ann died but 15 months later, in May 1747, Catherine gave birth to her sixth child, a son named Edward for his uncle. In March 1748, the death of seven-year-old Catherine left Edward and his elder sister Jane, aged eight, as the only surviving children. Then in May 1749 Avison and Edward's mother Ann died; she had been widowed for nearly 30 years and was probably around 70 years old. Only a week later, Catherine and Charles baptised another son, William. William was certainly named after his uncle in Hull, who was expanding his own family at this time; his wife Mary gave birth to a daughter, Ann, in 1744, and a son, William, in 1746.

~

In 1748, Avison gained an extra good source of income, although it required a considerable investment to secure it.

James Clark, the saddler who had replaced Avison as organist at St John's church, had died in 1743 and no successor had been appointed; the organ was allowed to fall into disrepair and in October 1748 it was described as 'long useless'. Enquiries were made about the possibility of renovations and a London organ builder offered to put it into playing order for £160 – a sum that suggests that considerable work was needed.

Avison was quick to scent an opportunity. He contacted the Corporation who provided the organist's salary. If the parishioners raised £60 towards the cost of repairs, he said, he would contribute the remaining £100 on condition that he was again appointed organist. As he continued to hold the St Nicholas' post, he would put in a suitable deputy who would need to be paid; even with this expense, he must have calculated that the income from the post would, over a period of years, allow him to recoup his investment and make a profit.

His financial situation must have been excellent to allow him to consider investing such a large amount of money. A genuine religious sentiment may also have motivated him, a wish to provide music for worship in the style he favoured, as opposed to that of Solomon Strolger at All Saints. But it is undoubtedly true that the businessman in him saw, and jumped at, a good chance to increase his income over the long-term.

~

The late 1740s were notable for the formation of two long-term friendships which were to influence Avison's personal and professional life for the next decade.

The first new friendship was with a young musician from Durham, John Garth. Garth was around 12 years younger than Avison and seems to have been in his mid-twenties when the two men met. He may have been a pupil of James Hesletine, organist of Durham Cathedral, and may have played in concerts in

Stockton around 1829. John Garth held concerts here, in the town centre.

Durham, which were run by Cathedral personnel. He was also organist of the church at Sedgefield, just outside Durham city.[62]

In 1745, aged 24, Garth seems to have decided to strike out on his own and held a concert in Race Week in Stockton on Tees. The following year he held Race Week concerts in both Stockton and Durham, which brought him into competition with the concerts put on by the Cathedral band in the latter place. He was very much at the start of his career and there is every evidence that he admired Avison greatly; he certainly played in Avison's concert band in Newcastle and in the next decade, the two men were to collaborate in a number of ways.

The other acquaintance was more in the nature of a patron. George Bowes of Gibside was the youngest of four brothers, but unexpectedly inherited his family's estates in County Durham and began an extensive programme of building and renovation. Avison's acquaintance with him may have begun as early as 1735; Bowes attended some of the original subscription concerts, and may have been one of the founding gentlemen.[63] But it was in the 1740s and particularly the latter part of the decade, that Avison began to benefit from the acquaintance. The accounts of Bowes and his second wife, Mary, are full of references to music, and to their patronage of Avison. In 1743, for instance, the Bowes attended Avison's Assize Week concert on August 3 and in May 1744 bought a copy of the Scarlatti concertos; they also patronised Garth's concerts in Stockton and Durham, and attended the Cathedral-run concerts in Durham.

The Bowes spent at least six months of the year, usually from the beginning of December to around May or June, in London where Bowes was a member of Parliament. Both attended musical events in the capital, including the playhouse, the opera and benefit concerts for their favourite musicians. Back home again in County Durham for the summer, the Bowes were disinclined to give up their musical entertainments, and threw open their home at Gibside to friends. In order to have a good band to perform their favourite pieces of music, they hired teachers to train the most musical of their servants; two footmen learned how to play the French horn and John Waltham, Bowes's valet, learned the violin. Claudius Heron, Bowes's factotum, was an excellent cellist, and in 1744 (and probably on other occasions too) the Bowes sent Heron and Waltham to play in Avison's and Garth's concerts, paying their travel expenses themselves.

GIBSIDE

The grand estate of Gibside in 1782.

The first time Avison is known to have visited Gibside was in May 1744. The reason for his visit is not known; he was paid the small sum of three shillings so it was clearly not a long visit – he may well have been asked to tune the harpsichord. In September of the same year he was back at Gibside for what may have been a longer visit for which he received payment of five guineas; he took with him copies of concertos by Geminiani and by the popular Sammartini, which the Bowes apparently wanted to buy.[64] The house would have been full of guests – friends and family of the Bowes; it is difficult to guess what Avison's position amongst them might have been, but his experiences with the Gilpin family in Cumberland and the gentlemen who founded the concerts would probably have made him easy in their company. In addition, many of the guests may have been his pupils. This would have been a gathering familiar to musicians working under the old patronage system.

1745 began, for everyone in the North East, in much the same way as usual. The Bowes attended Avison's Race Week concert in June and Garth's concerts in Stockton and Durham. But then the whole country was thrown into panic and confusion by the unexpected exploits of Bonnie Prince Charlie and the Jacobites. Supported by the goodwill of the French, the young Pretender sought to win back his grandfather's throne by raising the Highlands and marching south on London. The Prince and his followers got no further than Derby before suffering a crisis of confidence and retreating, despite the fact that a panic-struck capital was probably theirs for the taking. The Duke of Cumberland marched after them and, in early 1746, massacred the Jacobite army at Culloden.

George Bowes was one of the local landowners who raised an army to march for the Duke of Cumberland and defend the northern counties. But it was an anxious time for all concerned and Bowes was sufficiently uncertain of the outcome to instruct Claudius Heron to transport the Bowes plate and other valuables away from danger. In Newcastle, the rebellion must have been almost the sole topic of conversation; public entertainments such as Avison's subscription series would have seemed trivial by comparison.

It is likely that all such entertainments were cancelled while the outcome of the rebellion was in doubt and the disruption may have been considerable; early in 1746 Avison took the unprecedented step of advertising a second subscription series, suggesting that he needed to recoup lost income. Advertisements for the concerts appeared in the *Newcastle Courant* and the

Newcastle Journal at the end of February, and offered a series of six concerts – one a week (rather than the usual one a fortnight). Avison apologized for the short notice which prevented him from following the usual practice of approaching prospective subscribers in person: 'The shortness of the Time not allowing Mr Avison to make a personal Application to his Friends, he hopes they will excuse the Liberty of sending them Tickets, and those that don't chuse to subscribe need not return them.'

The notorious Duke of Cumberland who massacred the rebel Scots at Culloden in 1746.

The panic died quickly once the Duke of Cumberland wreaked havoc at Culloden. Public entertainments resumed in their usual form, the mid-year concerts and winter subscription series proceeding as normal. George Bowes sent his valet to play at Avison's Assize Week concert and to Garth's Race Week concert in Stockton.

Bowes was beginning to rely on Avison for more than musical entertainment. Increasingly, he was using him as a general agent, to buy supplies and pay bills in Newcastle. In December 1745, for instance, Avison brought the Bowes some ruled music-paper and paid a charitable donation on their behalf for the benefit of sick soldiers in the town; a year later, he was paying their bills for cambric and ruffles. In 1748, he dealt with orders for Irish linen for Bowes' shaving cloths, and damask linen for Bowes' nightcaps.

He was clearly becoming part of the Bowes's social circle. As the Bowes expanded the scale and ambition of their summer parties at Gibside, Avison was regularly invited. From 1746, the parties included not only local ladies and gentlemen but also the celebrated Italian violinist, Giuseppe Cattanei, who came so regularly that inventories of the house refer to 'Mr Cattanei's room'. Cattanei received 30 guineas for a stay of around two months over the summer; Avison was paid rather less, but nevertheless was clearly expected to stay several weeks; in 1744, he was paid five guineas, in 1745 eight guineas, and from 1746 ten guineas a year. Technically, Avison was as much an employee as any of the Bowes's servants, but the Bowes' accounts subtly distinguish the difference in social status by use of such formulae as 'paid Mr Avison for his trouble in coming to Gibside', suggesting that he was in some way obliging his patrons rather than merely obeying their orders.

The most splendid of these summer parties was that of 1750 when the Bowes staged an entire opera at Gibside. Maurice Green, an eminent composer patronised by the Bowes, had composed *Florimel* not for performance in the theatre but for private performance in the houses of the gentry and nobility; the work was ideally suited for precisely the type of party the Bowes held every summer. The servants and the Newcastle waits helped enlarge the band and Mrs Bowes herself sang the female lead. Avison had probably been employed in writing out the various parts for the band and was charged with ensuring that the waits turned up. Sadly, no account of the event survives.[65]

~

The connection with Bowes not only provided Avison with extra income but cemented his position as a cut above the average musician – no Newcastle wait would have been treated with such consideration or invited to stay. At the end of the 1740s, Avison was a well-off, well-established musician with a small but increasing reputation as a composer and with many influential friends. As he entered his forties, those friends were to take him in unexpected directions.

Increasing prosperity

'The entertainment of my subscribers'
Newcastle Courant September 14-21, 1751

A t the beginning of the 1750s, Avison was continuing to compose, and in September 1751 advertised the forthcoming Opus 3 – six concertos for a string band. The concertos were to be published in January 1751 and Avison was particularly keen to stress that there was an introduction which gave 'general Rules for Playing Instrumental Compositions in Parts but more, especially Calculated for the Use of this Work'.[66]

The introduction, which ran to five-and-a-half pages at the beginning of the work, was plainly intended to help the amateur performers who made up such a large part of Avison's own band and the bands of the Musical Societies who subscribed to the work. Much of this introduction was devoted to explaining a mark (the *Mostra*) of his own invention, designed to help players decipher the parts of the music; Avison said specifically that 'to lay down a complete system of Rules, is not my Intention', pointing out that in any case only 'a long and deep experience' could help performers to know how best to play.

Instead, he said, he merely offered 'some few Hints, which may be of Service in the performing of such Concertos'. Some of these hints were very basic, suggesting that the player should concentrate on keeping in tune, in time, and making sure he didn't play in the pauses. Avison also recommended watching the leader of the band for entries and advised the player not to forget the repeats. This was no doubt good advice for the amateur player, but some professional musicians took offence at what they took to be a lecture on how they should play.[67] William Hayes of Oxford described the presentation of the concertos as 'pompous'.

The concertos were dedicated to another of Avison's patrons, in this case a woman, Ann Ord. The Ord family were local landowners; John Ord and his younger brother William were both supporters of Avison and had been

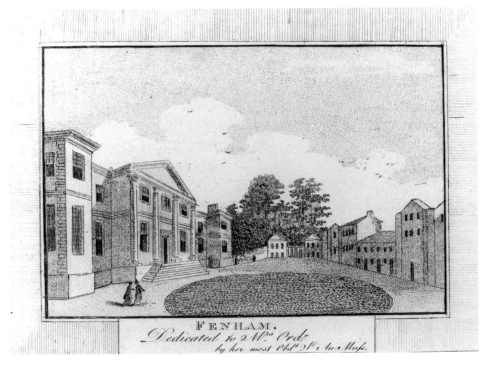

Fenham Hall, home of the Ord family, around 1785.

involved with setting up the subscription concerts in 1735. When John died in 1745, William inherited the estates and shortly afterwards married Ann Dillingham, the 20-year-old heiress to a rich London apothecary. Ann Ord was later a member of Elizabeth Montagu's blue-stocking group, skilled in performance (Avison called her playing 'elegant') and accustomed to discussing literary and philosophical matters with the best of her contemporaries. Like many other gentry families, the Ords spent winters in London and the summers in the North East; Avison frequently visited their house and was even on one occasion bought a hat by William Ord.

He followed up the Opus 3 concertos with another of his arrangements. In October 1751, he advertised the forthcoming winter series of concerts with one of his rare hints on the music to be performed.

'I cannot omit this opportunity of acquainting our Lovers of Music, that a generous Encourager of the Art has lately procured me, at his own Expense, all the Works of this Author.' The author in question was Jean-Philippe Rameau, a Frenchman best known for his operas and for his theories, based on

Enlightenment ideas, that the foundation of all music was harmony, which in turn was based on natural phenomena; harmony, Rameau believed, could be quantified and its rules found out and written down, in the same way that Newton had found out and set down the rules governing the planets. Avison's generous benefactor is unknown but might have been George Bowes – the Bowes admired Rameau and Mrs Bowes subscribed to his treatise on composition. The changes Avison made to Rameau's music may in fact have been minimal: a little rescoring to take account of the instruments available in the Newcastle concert band, some simplification of difficult passages. There was never any suggestion that these arrangement would be published which also suggests that the alterations may have been slight.

Composition made Avison better known in many areas throughout the country as music societies from Aberdeen to Nottingham bought his music, but, as was the case with all musicians, Avison's main daily concern was with the bread and butter source of his income – teaching. In November 1750, for the first and last time in his career, Avison published an advertisement for pupils. Generally, pupils (particularly for eminent teachers) were obtained by word of mouth; the fact that Avison advertised suggests that he was unexpectedly short of pupils or that he was changing the terms or conditions of his teaching.[68]

The advertisement makes it clear that Avison set aside Mondays and Fridays to teach in Newcastle and that his pupils usually went to his house in Rosemary Lane. (Wealthy patrons such as the Bowes would of course have expected him to go to their homes.) Avison seems to have adhered to the usual practice of seeing certain instruments as suitable only for men. Women were required to be elegant and decorous at all times; playing the violin required too energetic movements, playing wood-wind or brass instruments required unladylike puckering up of the face. Playing the cello, which required the player to place the instrument between the legs, was of course totally unacceptable for women, although one or two determined ladies were known to play 'side-saddle'. Suitable instruments for women were the harp and harpsichord which showed off graceful arm movements.

Avison therefore taught the harpsichord to young ladies in the morning between 9am and 1pm; gentlemen were taught the violin and flute from 2pm to 6pm in the afternoons. His charges were half a guinea entrance (the charge to be taken on as a pupil) and thereafter half a guinea per month or for eight lessons, which suggests that each pupil had two lessons a week, probably of half an hour each.

Avison's other regular job, as organist at St Nicholas' church, was apparently proceeding smoothly although in the middle of 1749, he became dissatisfied with the instrument, and decided it needed improving and modernisation. He particularly wanted to add a new swell stop. The Corporation would have to pay for any work and Avison cannily appealed to their civic pride. 'The stop,' he said, 'is now universally esteemed and made use of in most capital towns' and 'the addition of it to the organ of St Nicholas would make it one of the finest instruments in England'.[69]

He had his way. Bridges of London, who was still in Newcastle working on the organ of St John's, was authorised to do the work and Avison was told to negotiate a price with him. St John's was ready in September 1750 and the improvements to St Nicholas' organ finished two months later.

The money that Avison was beginning to amass seems to have been considerable. The safety of these savings was crucial; it was common for such savings to be lent to wealthy land owners who needed the money to provide cash flow, always a problem for wealthy families whose wealth was usually in buildings and property. In the 1740s, for instance, James Hesletine, organist of Durham Cathedral, invested £600 with George Bowes, receiving interest at $4\frac{1}{2}$%. Avison seems to have entrusted the bulk of his savings to William Ord; by March 1751, he had invested £50 which he lent to Ord at $4\frac{1}{2}$% interest, and by 1754 this had risen to £450, earning him a valuable £18 per annum.[70]

~

Domestically, the 1750s started as the 1740s had ended, with a mixture of good and bad times. Avison's and Catherine's youngest child, William, baptised only one week after the death of his grandmother, died in April 1750, at just 11 months old. Only five-year-old Jane and three-year-old Edward remained. Then Catherine gave birth for the eighth time, to another boy, called Charles for his father. Young Charles was to survive to adulthood, but the couple's last-born child, a daughter again called Catherine, born in November 1752, lived only four months.

There was a further family tragedy in these years. In Hull, Charles's elder brother William died in 1751, leaving his widow with a seven-year-old daughter and a six-year-old son. William left no will, suggesting that his death was sudden, and his brother Edward seems to have taken responsibility for the family although the widow and children continued living in Hull. Edward himself was prospering, saving money and investing it extensively in property, his financial situation perhaps helped by a lack of wife and children. Edward's investments included property in the Castle Garth and in Northumberland Street; he also lent money on mortgages and became Steward of the Taylor's Guild. William's place as organist of Holy Trinity, Hull was taken by one of Avison's pupils, Matthias Hawdon, who won an exacting election.

It is tempting to think that Avison's experiences with the early deaths of five of his eight children, and of his father and siblings, may have predisposed him to support a philanthropic undertaking that was promoted in Newcastle in the early 1750s. In 1751, a subscription was begun to set up a hospital, the Infirmary, for the poor of the region; this followed a similar trend in other large towns such as Bristol and York. Two of Avison's patrons, George Bowes and local magnate Sir Walter Blackett, were amongst six presidents chosen to head the organisation; any donors of £20 at any one time or more than two guineas annually were made Governors. There was wide enthusiasm for the venture and a number of fund-raising events were held: the physician Dr John Rotheram gave the proceeds of a lecture at Hexham, the theatre director Joseph Baker gave the profits of a play.

Avison decided to hold a benefit concert, the profits to be dedicated to the Infirmary. This was a new departure for Newcastle; concerts held for the

The Infirmary in 1753. It opened in October of that year at Forth Banks.

benefit of a charity were common elsewhere in the country but this was the first time a concert of this type had been held in the North East. Tickets were the usual 2s 6d each; the performers gave their services free and Avison himself bore the cost of heating and lighting the concert rooms. The concert raised £36 15s and was attended by 294 people; they heard, amongst other music, Avison's arrangements of Rameau's music.

The income from the concert was very similar to that raised from Mr Baker's play (£38) and Mr Rotheram's lecture (£42). Under the terms of the subscription it was pointed out that all three men should be made Governors of the Infirmary, but this did not happen, perhaps because it was considered that they had not contributed the whole money themselves. Avison was not put off and continued to support the Infirmary by holding concerts for its benefit in 1752, 1753 and 1754. But the amount raised consistently decreased from the £36 of the 1750 concert to £22 10s 6d in 1752, and only £13 4s 6d in 1753; the concerts may have ceased because they no longer raised significant amounts of money.

In addition to his regular, time-consuming activities, Avison was also engaged in a project that was different from anything he had tackled before. The idea had been suggested to him by some of the gentlemen who were his friends and patrons, particularly the gentlemen involved in the Newcastle Musical Society. These gentlemen were accustomed not only to play music but also to discuss philosophy and what was to become known as aesthetics. They had a predilection for big questions. What was music for? What should it sound like? Should music follow the precepts laid down by the ancient Greeks and Romans, as painting, sculpture and architecture had for many years? If so, what had the so-called 'ancient' music been like? Was vocal music more important than instrumental music and, if so, why?

Questions like these had interested musicians and scholars in Europe for some years and had been debated vehemently in speech and writing; in England, however, such matters were only just now beginning to attract attention. In 1752, encouraged by the gentlemen and spurred on by his own enthusiasm, Avison produced the first book in English on these important new ideas – *An Essay on Musical Expression*.

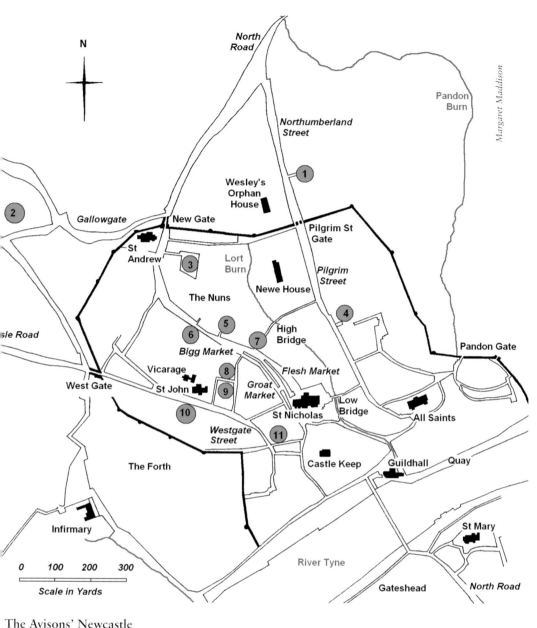

The Avisons' Newcastle

1 Lisle Street, home of Charles Avison's son Charles in 1795

2 Spring Gardens, music garden

3 Green Court, Charles Avison's last home from 1763-1770

4 Bell's Court, home of Charles Avison's grandson Charles and his family

5 Turk's Head assembly room

6 Avison's birthplace on Newgate Street

7 Humble's Buildings, the Avisons' family home 1730s-1740s

8 Rosemary Lane

9 Lying-In Hospital

10 Assembly Room on Westgate Street

11 Back Row

St Nicholas' church from Side, 1808.

Charles Avison, painted by Charles Lindo, 1761.

Perspective View of Newcaſ

Newcastle upon Tyne around 1746, engraved for *The Complete English Traveller*. St John's church is just to the left of the Castle Keep, and St Nicholas' church with its lantern spire dominates the view. To the right is the spire of All Saints.

...Tyne, in Northumberland.

The town wall still extends along the quayside as far east as Sandgate, but would soon be demolished. The Tyne Bridge dated from medieval times and would be swept away by disastrous floods in 1771, the year after Charles Avison's death.

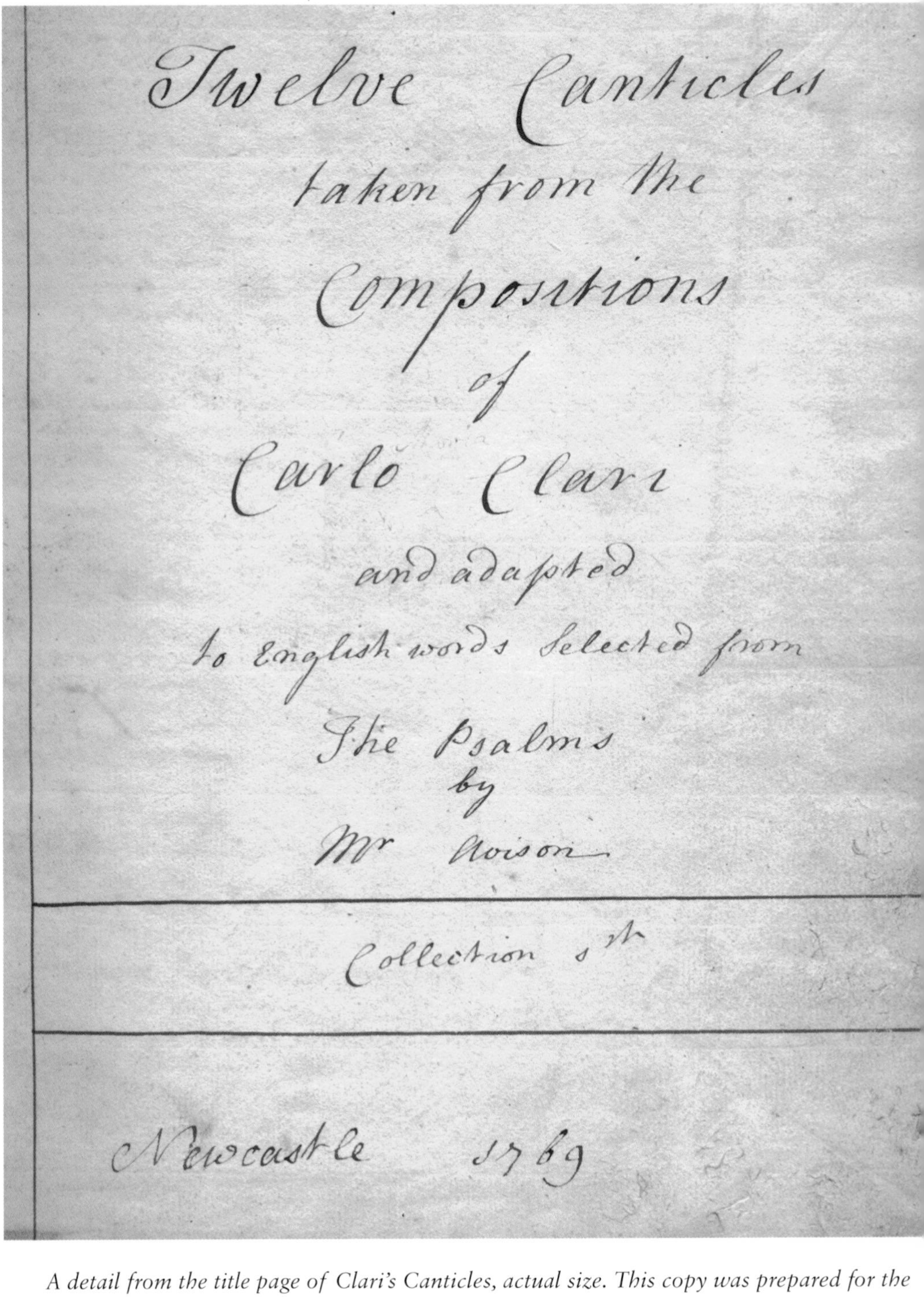

Twelve Canticles

taken from the

Compositions

of

Carlo Clari

and adapted

to English words selected from

The Psalms
by

Mr Avison

Collection 5th

Newcastle 1769

A detail from the title page of Clari's Canticles, actual size. This copy was prepared for the printer partly by Avison in his own hand (seen here) and partly by an assistant.

The second canticle, slightly smaller than actual size, in Avison's neat hand, ready for the printer.

7

Francesco Geminiani, Avison's London teacher, holding a copy of Corelli's concerti grossi open at concerto no. VIII. Oil on canvas by Andrea Soldi, c1735.

The Lock Hospital, Hyde Park Corner, London, pictured here in the 19th century, was part of Christ's Hospital. It was opened in 1747 and was the first specialist hospital for venereal diseases. Avison composed music performed in aid of the Lock Hospital in 1765.

Newcastle's Infirmary, 1786. Avison held benefit concerts in aid of the Infirmary which opened in October 1753.

Avison Ensemble founder, Gordon Dixon, at Sotheby's Auction House on May 17, 2002, having just successfully purchased Avison's Second Workbook for £21,510 (the hammer price was £18,000).

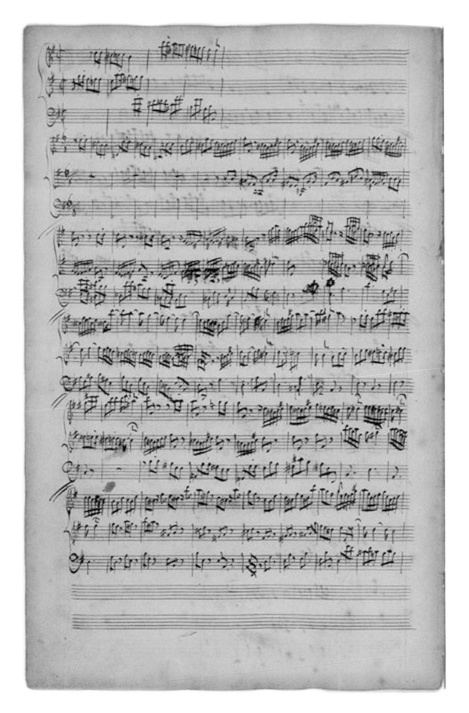

A page from Charles Avison's Concerto in E minor, Opus 6, No 8, allegro. It shows the moment of creativity as the composition is set down on the page.

Top, the Avison tomb at St Andrew's church, Newcastle. The stone dates from 1890.

Below, the Avison Society plaque at St Andrew's, unveiled by the Lord Mayor in 1994.

Putting pen to paper

'A few observations on that delightful Art', Charles Avison, An Essay on Musical Expression, 1752

Avison's book may have been born out of learned discussions amongst well-educated gentlemen but when he came to put his ideas in writing, he decided to write for the intelligent layman who had little or no practical musical expertise. 'As the public Inclination for Music seems every Day advancing,' he began, 'It may not be amiss, at this Time, to offer a few Observations on that delightful Art.' Mindful of this lay audience, he prefaced the book with a brief glossary, defining basic musical terms such as melody, harmony, modulation, cadences and graces.[71]

The book is perhaps a little disjointed, covering a variety of topics ranging from the theoretical (the

AN

ESSAY

ON

MUSICAL EXPRESSION.

By CHARLES AVISON,
Organist in NEWCASTLE.

Sò ben, ch'era Meſtier da Virtuoſi
La Muſica una Volta ; e l'imparavano,
Tra gl' huomini i più grandi, ei più famoſi.
Sò che Davidde, e Socrate cantavano ;
E che de l'Arcade, il Greco, e lo Spartano
D'altra Scienza al par la celebravano.
Sò, che fù di Miracoli feconda,
E che ſapea ritor l'Anime à Lete,
Benche fuſſero quaſi in ſu la Sponda.
SALVAT. ROSA. Sat. I.

LONDON:
Printed for C. DAVIS, oppoſite *Gray's-Inn-Gate*,
in *Holborn.* MDCCLII.

effect music has on the listener, for instance) to the purely practical (when to add ornaments to a performance). Avison attempts to impose order on his material by dividing the book into three parts. Part One covers general matters, Part Two deals with composition and Part Three with performance. Each part is then sub-divided into two or three sections.

The first section of Part One deals with the 'force and effect' of music. Avison wanted to explore the effect music has on the listener. 'It is of mighty Efficacy,' he wrote, 'in working both on his imagination and his Passions.' By 'passions' he meant 'emotions'; music, he felt, has an unparalleled ability to rouse good emotions and to banish bad emotions. It 'pour[s] in upon the Mind, a silent and serene Joy, beyond the Power of Words to express, and to fix the Heart in a rational, benevolent and happy Tranquility.'

This effect, he said, is strengthened when assisted by the main topic of the book – *Musical Expression*. Oddly, he nowhere defined what he meant by this term, perhaps because it was something he felt could not be expressed in words, but could only be experienced. For this, a listener needed only good taste and judgement, and a wide experience in listening to good music.

In the second section of Part One, Avison described music by relating it to painting. He may have been influenced in this by his friendship with John Brown, who was a keen amateur painter, and in addition many of his local patrons – the Ords, the Ridleys, and Bowes – were building up art collections which Avison would have seen and discussed; an analogy between music and art was not original, however, and had been raised elsewhere. Nevertheless, Avison felt that the comparison would help his readers understand music more effectively. 'As musical Composition is known to very few beside the Professors and Composers of Music themselves,' he wrote, 'it may not be amiss to draw out some of the most striking of [the] Analogies [between music and painting]; and by this Means, in some Degree at least, give the common Reader an idea of musical Composition'.

In Part Two, Avison tackled his favourite topic: composition. He was convinced that the best music showed a balance between three important factors: melody (which he called 'air'), harmony, and musical expression. He devoted considerable space to discussing the music of specific composers, many of whom, he felt, had stressed one of these three factors at the expense of the others, and also condemned composers and performers who indulged in virtuosic showiness – anathema to Avison and his belief in simplicity as preached by his old teacher, Geminiani.

His contempt fell principally on composers like Vivaldi ('defective in various Harmony and true Invention'). On the other hand, he praised Palestrina (the 'Father of Harmony') and, unsurprisingly, Geminiani, Scarlatti ('bold and inventive'), Corelli ('faultless') and Rameau ('graceful and spirited'). He was more reserved about the darling of the age, George Frederic Handel, but enthused about his 'Manly style' and 'noblest Harmonies'.

Part Three of the *Essay* is in effect a reprint, slightly altered, of the Preface to Opus 3, dealing with advice to the performer. Avison also discussed the idea of imitation, one of the topics interesting continental scholars. Should music imitate the natural world, particularly in a literal sense as in Vivaldi's *Four Seasons*, where amongst other things, the strings imitate the barking of a dog? Indulging in a moment of wit, Avison advised such composers to 'follow the much more effectual Method of introducing the Creatures themselves'.

The readers of the *Essay* were not expected to take the more contentious points on trust. Avison included many footnotes (including, for instance, a discussion of contemporary church music), and quoted extended extracts from many other authors on the subject, including classical authors such as Polybius and Horace, continental authors such as Montesquieu, Calmet and Bonet, and English writers such as John Brown and Sir William Temple. The extensive range of materials used in the *Essay* suggests that Avison was a widely-read man, even if some of the sources may originally have been drawn to his attention by his well-educated patrons; he is known to have subscribed to a number of publications including music, volumes of poetry and sermons, and a book of voyages, and may well have exchanged copies of books with friends.

In addition, there were a number of other places where Avison may have obtained information and ideas. The Thomlinson Library was an impressive collection of over 1,600 books kept at St Nicholas' church and available for parishioners to borrow. (Avison donated a copy of the *Essay* to this library.) For new works and lighter reading matter, he could have used the commercial circulating library set up by Joseph Barber in 1746, or a rival library run by stationer William Charnley

ten years later. To what extent he could read non-English works in their original languages is not clear but he may well have picked up some Italian from Geminiani, and his comments on Rameau suggest that he may have read the composer's book on harmony before it appeared in an English translation.

The *Essay on Musical Expression* was published in London, by C. Davis in Holborn, in early 1752; Avison advertised it in local papers in April. It is unlikely that he anticipated the storm of protest that it provoked. What must have seemed, to Avison and his friends, an unexceptional discussion of a gentlemanly topic, received a vitriolic response in some quarters.

Objections to the book were embodied in a volume that came out early in 1753, entitled *Remarks on Mr Avison's Essay on Musical Expression*; the author was William Hayes, Professor of Music at Oxford, and devotee of George Frederic Handel. Hayes was evidently a pleasant man, but with a grudge and a quill pen in hand he could be vicious. His opinions differed from Avison's in several respects. They had diametrically opposing views on so-called ancient music, Avison being in favour of studying it and allowing its influence, Hayes being adamant against it. Hayes hated modern church-music, whereas Avison made a number of cutting remarks about the old style that Hayes favoured. Avison praised Italian church music, particularly the psalms of Benedetto Marcello, but Hayes, a fervent nationalist who felt that the Church of England should only be served by English music, thought these degenerate.[72] Avison's greatest fault in Hayes's eyes, however, was that he had been lukewarm in his praise of Hayes's idol, Handel, who was, despite his German origin, an icon of English nationalism.

Hayes was prepared to be brutal in his defence of composers and principles he held dear. He began his *Remarks* by trying to cast doubt on Avison's credibility as a composer, attacking his compositions as incorrect in harmony and musical technique, clearly trying to imply that Avison's writings on music were not credible. Then he indulged in a few brisk remarks on Avison's character; only after this did he tackle specific points raised in the *Essay* – even then, his tone throughout was one of scorn.

Stung, Avison swiftly penned a reply which was published as a separate pamphlet in April 1753, lightly disguised as a letter to an unnamed friend in London. He said that he did not intend to indulge in a slanging match with Hayes, but nevertheless could not resist describing him as a 'virulent, though … not formidable' opponent.[73] Hayes, Avison claimed, had totally misunderstood the aim of the *Essay*. It was not intended to be a musical textbook but an examination of music 'from the School of Nature and Good Sense'. He suggested that Hayes had for some reason a personal grudge against him, defended his compositional principles, fended off criticism of Marcello and other Italian composers, and took great pleasure in pointing out that some of the compositional 'faults' of which Hayes had accused him had also been committed by Hayes's idol, Handel.

Handel, from Hawkins' General History of the Science and Practice of Music, 1776.

With regard to Hayes's favourite, Handel, Avison said, was 'exalted' and 'harmonious' with 'abilities equal to every Thing' and 'Genius capable of soaring the boldest Flights'. He had only one fault; he had composed too much under commercial pressures and had occasionally produced some inferior music 'to suit the vitiated Taste of the Age'. His virtues were far more numerous than his vices, however, and while he was not perfect, he was a 'glorious Example of those amazing Powers that actuate the human Soul'. Avison had on a number of occasions performed Handel's music and continued to do so; nonetheless, the idea that he disliked the German has persisted.

In June 1753, Avison reprinted his reply to Hayes, the revised text of the *Essay* and a letter written to him by a clergyman about the music of the ancients, all in one volume. He had given as good as he had got with every appearance of relish. But the furore over the *Essay* seemed to set the tone for the new decade; the 1750s were to be an argumentative and difficult time. After the apparently near-effortless professional rise in the 1740s, he was to face increasing problems – some large, some small – both in Newcastle and outside it. In 1753, as the second edition of the *Essay* became available, these difficulties were already manifesting themselves in Durham.

Confrontations

'The organist at Newcastle joyns his forces with all his Myrmidons'
Spencer Cowper, November 26, 1752

In Durham, John Garth was prospering. His Race Week concerts were apparently popular and well-supported even though they had to compete with concerts put on by the Cathedral personnel; his teaching practice – always the mainstay of any musician's income – was expanding considerably. Amongst others, he taught the cello to the children of Lord Barnard at Raby Castle, near Staindrop, and harpsichord to the Milbankes at Halnaby in Yorkshire. The Bowes of Gibside continued to support him, occasionally sending their servants to play in his concert band and attending the concerts themselves; although he was clearly never so much a favourite with the Bowes as Avison, he was obviously much admired. His cello playing was of a very high standard, as evidenced by the cello concertos he wrote for his own performance and which still survive.

Garth's friendship with Avison was still close; they used the same band for their concerts and played in each other's entertainments. Both men had friends and supporters amongst the prebendaries at Durham Cathedral and were often to be found together at dinner parties, following a pleasant dinner with a little music-making. The organist of Durham Cathedral, James Hesletine – nearly 30 years Avison's elder – was also a guest on many of these occasions but other dinner guests noted that he generally refused to join in the music-making. According to the Dean of the Cathedral, Spencer Cowper, Hesletine disliked Avison, seeing him as a competitor. Hesletine was an irascible man, and Avison seems to have done nothing to provoke him.[74]

In 1752, however, Avison and John Garth were party to a scheme that led to a serious confrontation with Hesletine, with the long-established Cathedral-run series of winter concerts, and with the clerics of the Cathedral, Spencer Cowper chief amongst them. The scheme originated with a number of gentlemen who were Garth's patrons and grew out of a genuine desire to advance him professionally. Some of the gentlemen, including Lord Barnard of Raby Castle, and very possibly George Bowes of Gibside, suggested that they would finance a winter series of concerts which Garth would direct and from which he would take the profits.

It was natural that Garth should consult his friend Charles Avison; Avison was an experienced concert promoter – by this time he had run Newcastle concerts for 17 years. Avison agreed to play in the concerts and to bring with him the players of the Newcastle band. The financing gentlemen also agreed to play in the concerts. Avison may have helped to choose repertoire and to direct some of the music.

The major problem was the location of the series. Inevitably it was to be held in Durham where Garth lived but this brought it directly into conflict with the already existing winter series of concerts run by Cathedral personnel. There was a danger that the two series might divide the audience for music to such an extent that neither series was viable. To counteract this, Avison and Garth seem to have adopted an expedient that they hoped would encourage music-lovers to attend both series. The Cathedral concerts concentrated on the older repertoire, presenting music by composers such as Geminiani, Corelli and – the universal favourite in Durham – Handel; these were composers (particularly the first two) that Avison admired but he and Garth nevertheless abandoned them for a more modern repertoire, including music by Avison himself, Rameau (presumably in the form of Avison's arrangements) and Felice Giardini, an Italian violinist newly arrived in London and at that moment the toast of music-lovers in the capital.

Their problems really began, however, when they came to look for a vocal soloist for the series. Newcastle churches had no real choirs, using only charity school children and a few adult singers where necessary; the main emphasis was always on congregational singing. There were no professional singers in the town. Whenever Avison needed a singer, he either applied to the theatre actresses, or hired a singer from Durham Cathedral. His first soloist, Thomas Mountier, had long since succumbed to drink and no longer sang in public; Avison had since used, with James Hesletine's permission, one of the boy choristers from the Cathedral.

Avison and Garth therefore applied to the Cathedral again to find a singer for their concerts. They seem to have been genuinely surprised to encounter considerable hostility. The organisers of the Cathedral-run concerts saw the

Durham, 1745, from Wm Hutchinson's History and Antiquities of Durham.

new series as a threat which needed to be quashed at the earliest possible opportunity; Hesletine (who directed the Cathedral concerts) was particularly outraged. So was the Dean; Spencer Cowper at once issued a stern warning to all the singing men and choristers that no collaboration with Avison and Garth would be tolerated.

His hostility was so great that Cowper refused to go to Avison and Garth's first Durham concert, on December 6, 1752. He wanted to know what happened, however, so he sent his wife and her companion to the lunchtime rehearsal and the evening concert. Her report, and the copy of the programme she brought back, had him crowing in triumph. He enjoyed decrying the modern music played (although Mrs Cowper told him that the players were excellent), casting scorn on all 'new' music as a matter of principle. In addition, his wife had reported that the audience was almost entirely made up of women owing to ticket conditions which meant that gentlemen subscribers could transfer them only to women (and two women at that, as no woman would go to a public event alone); as most of the gentlemen played in the band and transferred their tickets to their wives and daughters, this ensured an almost entirely female audience. Cowper thought this another great cause for derision. Cowper, the prebendaries, Hesletine and the singing men were all exuberant. Garth's series, they thought, could not possibly survive.

They were wrong. Avison and Garth proceeded happily throughout the winter with their concerts and planned another series for the following year.

The enmity between the series developed into full-blown rivalry. In search of a novelty that might attract audiences away from Avison and Garth's series, the Cathedral personnel decided to put on outdoor concerts, a risky venture in view of the vagaries of the weather. In June 1753 and 1754, the choir removed themselves to the gardens at Old Durham just outside the city, and the concerts were popular enough with the ladies and gentlemen for Garth to copy them in May 1755. The choir then retaliated in 1756 with a series of four concerts, two held on the river itself and on the banks, the other two held in the Cathedral. These latter concerts were unprecedented as concerts were generally considered too trivial for performance in churches. The inclusion of extracts from Handel's oratorios was probably used to justify the unusual step and the review in the Newcastle papers indulged in a little snobbery at the expense of the more secular repertoire of Avison and Garth's concerts, remarking that 'the solemnity of the Pieces inspired the Hearers with an awful Kind of Satisfaction, infinitely superior to the Pleasure experienced by lighter Pieces'.

Garth in turn offered international soloists at his concerts; his July concert in 1753 was notable for the personal appearance of the Italian violinist, Felice Giardini, who was probably spending the summer with the Bowes. Avison may have been present at Gibside when a scandal broke over the head of Giardini. Giardini and the singer Violante Vestris were found in bed together by George Bowes; to appease his fury, they insisted that they had been married in secret in London. Bowes believed them, but Harriet Lane Fox of Bramham Park in Yorkshire, who was also staying at Gibside, did not, and insisted upon them marrying

Felice Giardini, 1716-1796.

'again'. This may have been Avison's first encounter with Giardini, who was to become a great friend; if so he clearly did not think any the worse of him for the escapade.[75] For Giardini, it was the start of a 20-year association with midsummer concerts in the North East; he and Avison were to become particularly friendly and were to collaborate in later years on at least one compositional project. Presumably, Avison thought Giardini not prone to the faults of virtuosi performers that he had condemned in the *Essay*.

At some point after 1751, Avison also acted as Giardini's agent in the purchase of a violin that had once belonged to Corelli. This violin, dating from 1683, had come into the possession of an Englishman residing in Italy, William Corbett, who bequeathed this and other instruments to Gresham College. The college refused the bequest however and in 1751 the instruments were sold. The Corelli violin was bought by an unknown gentleman living in Newcastle and it was from this gentleman that Avison bought the violin on Giardini's behalf.[76]

The problem of a vocal soloist for the series had still not been resolved and in 1754, Avison and Garth made another attempt to obtain a singer from the Cathedral. In view of the hostility displayed by the Cathedral personnel, this would at first sight seem to have had little chance of success; however, Avison was well acquainted with one of the men he and Garth approached and they may have felt that a personal appeal might succeed.

The singing man in question was Cornforth Gelson, a County Durham man who had started his musical career as a chorister at Durham Cathedral. When his voice broke, he had taken up a post as wait in Newcastle and as such must have played in Avison's concerts and became well acquainted with him, before, after only four years in Newcastle, he returned to the Cathedral as an adult singing man. Gelson was indeed interested in singing in the new concerts, as was one of the senior choristers, Stephen Paxton.

The Dean, Spencer Cowper, sprang into action with martial fervour. Stephen Paxton clearly thought discretion the better part of valour and went off to London where he was to make a name, and a fortune, as a cellist and composer. Gelson was not as fortunate. Cowper used an illegitimate child as an excuse to dismiss him. Gelson, his wife and two children found themselves destitute and it was a year before a new job was found in Edinburgh.

The extent to which Avison was involved in the organisation and running of his friend's Durham series is not easy to discover. He certainly played in the concerts and had some say in what music was performed. Spencer Cowper and

James Hesletine regarded him as one of the prime movers. But as the series went on, apparently with some success, into the middle and late 1750s, Avison may well have withdrawn from any detailed involvement in the series, even if he continued to play in the concerts themselves. He had pressing concerns of his own in Newcastle.

For the first time since the affair of the Swiss violinist, he was facing opposition to his directorship of the Newcastle concert series.

A competitor

'An unlucky Difference ... betwixt him and Mr Avison'
Newcastle Journal December 9-16, 1758

In Newcastle, Avison's life had continued in much its usual vein during the early part of the 1750s. After penning and publishing his sharp reply to William Hayes, and his second edition of the *Essay* in 1753, he settled back to his customary routine of the winter subscription series, the mid-year Race and Assize Week concerts and the benefit for the Infirmary; these latter benefits were dropped in 1755 but Avison and his brother Edward became official Visitors or inspectors to the Infirmary.[77] His income was still steadily improving; in 1754 or thereabouts he transferred his savings to the Old South Sea Annuities, stock that produced an income of around £30 per annum. Avison, however, had no bank account so William Ord cashed his interest bills on the bank on his behalf.[78]

Avison was settled in Newcastle but in all probability still travelled quite frequently; his visits to Gibside are well documented, but from 1755 comes one of the rare pieces of evidence that he travelled further afield. In this year he travelled south to Cambridge, probably to see the poet Thomas Gray; he may have performed either publicly or privately, as he was later able to attract Cambridge subscribers to his publications.[79]

Avison was particularly active compositionally, producing three large-scale works, Opus 4, 5 and 6. The eight concertos of Opus 4, which were published in 1755, had almost certainly been performed in the Newcastle concerts before publication and were dedicated to Avison's pupil and patron, Lady Milbanke.[80] Sir Ralph Milbanke of County Durham and Halnaby in Yorkshire, was a major landowner and MP for Scarborough; his wife, Elizabeth, was the daughter of the MP for Durham and an excellent harpsichord player, taking part in the select private concerts held in London by Harriet Lane Fox.

In 1756 the six sonatas of Opus 5 were dedicated to another patron, Lady Blackett, wife of local magnate Sir Walter Blackett. The Blacketts were the

Sir Walter Blackett, a very important and wealthy man in Newcastle in the mid-18th century. He owned the Newe House, pictured on page 14.

leading family in Newcastle although in the late 1720s the family had nearly died out in the male line and was only rescued by Sir Walter Calverley who had succeeded his uncle on condition he took the name of Blackett and married his illegitimate cousin, Elizabeth. Sir Walter was several times elected MP for Newcastle and was also its mayor on several occasions. Avison may have visited this family too, in addition to the Bowes and Ord families, for musical parties. The sonatas, for harpsichord, two violins and cello, are unusual in that the harpsichord part is written out in full rather than sketched out with a bass line and figures upon which the player could improvise; this argues that Avison saw the part as more important than in the usual run of such works.

In 1757, Avison produced another of his arrangements, this time for use in church. Local bookseller, William Charnley, was publishing an edition of Isaac Watts's psalms, for use both in the home and in church. Such books appeared frequently but generally were words only; Charnley's edition was the first known edition to be published in the North East with tunes included. Avison took the opportunity to make a practical demonstration of his views on music suitable for worship, presenting 43 tunes in very simple, unornamented versions, with tune and bass line only.[81]

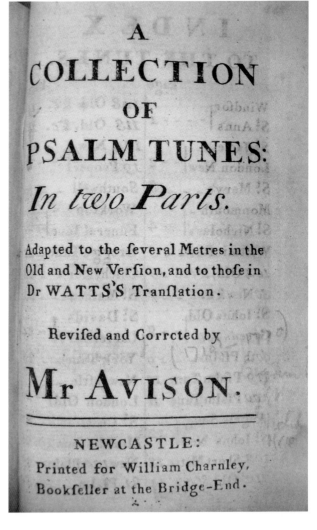

A
COLLECTION
OF
PSALM TUNES:
In two Parts.

Adapted to the several Metres in the Old and New Version, and to those in Dr WATTS'S Translation.

Revised and Corrected by

Mr AVISON.

NEWCASTLE:
Printed for William Charnley, Bookseller at the Bridge-End.

Opus 6, consisting of 12 more concertos for a string band, appeared in March 1758. This was not an entirely new composition for it incorporated works from revisions and additions to Opus 2 together with four new concertos. It has been suggested that Avison was following a tradition adhered to by his teacher, Geminiani, and his teacher, Corelli of producing an Opus 6 that represented the best of his compositional output – rather in the manner of an apprentice who has to produce a masterpiece to be recognised as a master of his craft. At the age of 49, Avison may have felt at the peak of his powers. In the same year he also issued his Opus 3, 4 and 6 as *Twenty Six Concertos … in Score for the use of Performers on the Harpsichord*. Avison had emphasised in the *Essay* the importance of the publication of the concertos in score – with all the parts visible to the performer – in encouraging players to consider the work as a whole. In this too, Avison was influenced by Geminiani, who had recently published some of his own works in a similar form.

One project had, however, been put aside. Avison had planned to transcribe the psalms of Italian composer, Benedetto Marcello, as a practical demonstration of his views on the theory of music, but this turned out to be one project too many.[82] He persuaded John Garth to take it on. The first volume of Garth's arrangements appeared in 1757 and Avison provided the preface, talking at length about the principles which ought to be observed in church music. Oddly, given the bad feeling between Garth and the Cathedral personnel caused by the rival subscription series, copies of the psalms were bought by the Bishop of Durham, the Dean, Spencer Cowper, the choir (who bought two copies, presumably for performance purposes) and even James Hesletine. In Newcastle, Avison and some friends set up a Marcello Society to sing the music, albeit privately rather than in public; in a letter written in October 1758, he told a friend in Oxford that there were nine members of the Society, many of whom had not previously been used to singing at all. His best singer, he said, was Ann Ord, 'whose voice is a strong and melodius Contra alto with Compass sufficient to lead also in the Cantos'.[83]

But trouble was brewing in precisely the area where Avison probably felt most secure: in his running of the subscription series. He had been both its financial and musical director for 20 years and, since the contretemps with the Swiss violinist, without any hint of trouble or competition. In late 1757, however, he faced both criticism from the subscribers to the concerts, and the possibility of a serious competitor.

Visiting musicians had come and gone without any controversy or ill-feeling during Avison's ascendancy in the town, except for one short-lived episode in 1741 when a visiting Welsh harper had put his small audience down to critical comments made by jealous rivals; this may, however, have been an attempt to save face. Most visitors plainly enjoyed their stay and found it sufficiently profitable to want to return. Felice Giardini played in mid-year concerts in Durham and Newcastle year after year; the Hungarian clarinettist, Mr Charles, lingered in the North East for several months in 1754-5, playing in the subscription series in both Newcastle and Durham and holding benefit concerts of his own, before moving on to Hexham. Neither of these threatened Avison's position as organiser of the subscription series.

The first sign of trouble came in late 1757; the winter series was plainly not entirely on a sound financial basis. Interestingly, it was at about this time that the Durham series run by Avison and Garth also suffered financially, doubts being expressed as to whether it could carry on. The difficulties coincided with the start of the Seven Years' War, sparked by confrontations in America and hostilities in Europe between Austria and Prussia. In times of war, public entertainment often suffered, owing to a widespread feeling that such things were too trivial for serious times.

In October 1757, Avison was forced to put up the cost of tickets to the series, a clear indication that income was not keeping pace with expenditure. The cost of subscribing to the entire series went up, by about 25%, from 10s 6d (half a guinea) to 13 shillings, and the cost of individual tickets by around 20%, from 2s 6d to three shillings. Avison justified the rise by suggesting that subscribers were getting more value for their money. 'As the Room will be illuminated with Wax Lights, to give more Elegance to the Concert, it is hoped the Advance of the Tickets on that Account, will not be disapproved by the Subscribers.' This eloquence hides the fact that the rise was probably forced upon him by the Directors of the Assembly Rooms; expensive wax candles did less damage to the decorations than did cheaper tallow candles.[84]

Early in 1758, Avison embarked on a new venture. In addition to the winter series, he now offered a summer series of concerts: five concerts to be held on the first Thursday of every month from April until August. These five concerts were to cost as much as the winter series had originally cost: half a guinea for the entire series or three shillings for individual tickets. Avison must have thought there was a market for such concerts and history shows that his judgement on such matters was usually excellent. But the timing suggests that another source of income was not unwelcome.

In July, Avison welcomed Italian violinist Felice Giardini to his Assize Week concert; the audience was evidently 'very full and splendid' and 'expressed the greatest Satisfaction on hearing the Performance of the Ingenious and celebrated Signior Giardini'. He was, however, less than enthusiastic about the arrival in Newcastle of another visitor, a young Irishman, Charles Claget.

Claget was probably around 18 years old when he arrived in the town in the summer of 1758 and was clearly ambitious, and eager to find a town where he could establish himself. As was customary, he placed an advertisement in local papers to announce that he was opening a school, offering tuition in dancing, the violin, cello and guitar as well as other instruments. There were plenty of other music teachers in town and Avison was probably sufficiently well-established with enough pupils not to fear a competitor in this area; what really seems to have alarmed him were Claget's proposed ventures into concert promotion.

It was normal practice for visitors to the area to put on a benefit concert, which helped to raise money and to advertise their teaching practice. Avison had never had cause to concern himself over concerts by Giardini, Charles the Hungarian clarinettist, or other visitors such as Italian singer Christina Passerini who had spent a week or two in Newcastle in 1752 on her way south from Edinburgh to London.[85] But Claget seems to have had his sights set on something more ambitious; although he later took care to deny the suggestion, he may have been contemplating running a subscription series in Newcastle. Given the continuing rivalry between the two series in Durham, Claget must have touched a sore spot.

By his own account (in a paragraph attached to an advertisement for a concert in December 1758), Claget held two concerts in Newcastle over the summer, although advertisements for these do not survive. Then disaster struck in the shape of what Claget described as an 'unlucky Difference ... betwixt him and Mr Avison'. The subject of this 'difference' is not clear but Avison was clearly not the only person who suspected Claget's intentions, for Claget admitted that 'some people misjudging Mr Claget's Intention, have taken Publication of a Concert as an Opposition'. Claget pleaded for understanding, saying that 'this is not a Subscription Concert, but one Benefit-Night, what is commonly granted to any Performers, tho' they stay not a Week on the Spot'.

For the BENEFIT of Mr CLAGET.

AT Mr Parker's Long-room, on Monday the 18th Inftant, will be perform'd

A CONCERT of VOCAL and INSTRUMENTAL MUSIC.

To begin exactly at Seven o'Clock.

Tickets to be had at Mr Parker's, Mr Steel's, the Exchange Coffee-houfe, and of Mr Claget, in Silver ftreet, at 3 s. each.

N. B. As fome Perfons misjudge Mr Claget's Intention, and takes the Publication of a Concert as an Oppofition; he defires they would not look on it in fuch a Light for the future, but con-fider Mufic is his Profeffion, that this is not a Subfcription, but a fingle Benefit-night, and what Newcaftle, as well as all other great Towns, have granted to Strangers who ftay'd not a Week with them; further, that he had two before the unlucky Difference hap-pened betwixt him and Mr Avifon, and always propofed having one in the Winter, and one in the Summer; the Truth of which he dare fay Mr Avifon will juftify to the Curious: And further, this Difference caufed a Delay, or he propofed having it above a Month fooner.

PETER R——

Charles Claget's advertisement, Newcastle Courant, December, 16, 1758.

He had, he said, always intended to have two benefits, one in the summer and one in winter; Avison, he claimed, knew this and had not expressed any objection until that 'unlucky Difference'.

The fact that Claget had picked on Newcastle as an ideal place to start his career suggests that musical life in the town was well-known for its vibrancy and for offering opportunities to an enterprising and dynamic young man. But it is significant that his presence clearly worried Avison more than any other musician ever had; he had arrived at a particularly sensitive time when Avison's dominance of the winter subscription series was being seriously challenged.

Trouble blew up around the most apparently trivial of matters – an apparent change to one of the conditions governing the subscription tickets. When the series had been originally set up, over 20 years previously, a subscription ticket admitted to the concert either the gentleman who bought it, or two ladies of his family. Evidently, over the years, strict enforcement of this condition had lapsed, and subscribers fell into the habit of transferring tickets to other men.

This was not a small matter, for if two men shared a ticket in this way, it generally meant the loss of the sale of another ticket. In 1758, Avison attempted to enforce the condition, indicating that he thought it a significant matter which was losing him a considerable amount of money. There were immediate objections, with claims that he was trying to impose a new and unjust condition on the tickets. Confusion then arose over conditions attached to other tickets, including the 'double-ticket' which carried two names and admitted either of the Subscribers or two ladies, and the 'Single-Ticket' which could indeed be transferred to another gentleman, but only within the subscriber's family.

Matters were not improved when Avison fell ill just before the series began and was therefore unable to visit potential subscribers as he usually did, and explain the situation. Instead he was forced to write a long letter to the *Newcastle Journal* to set out his point of view; this appeared in early November 1758.[86] In the letter, he set out the history of the series, detailing how the ticket conditions had evolved, and insisting that his own actions were only reinstating the original position. But he also felt the need to include a long justification, both of the need for a subscription series in the town and of his own management of the concerts. It appears that doubts had been raised on both points.

As far as the subscription series itself was concerned, Avison insisted that 'Public Music was of public Utility'. In short, it was not mere trivial entertainment, or an expendable luxury but of real value to the community. It had three benefits: firstly, it brought 'the genteeler People' into town and thus helped to promote trade as they spent money on lodgings, food etc; secondly, it acted as a social facilitator, improving 'the social and benevolent Affections, by the general Intercourse of Friends and Acquaintances'; thirdly, the fact that Newcastle had subscription concerts, conducted with 'Decorum', gave visitors to the town a favourable impression of its people and facilities.

Moving on to his own management of the series, Avison pointed out that he had devoted a great deal of time and effort to conducting the concerts; moreover, he said, he had always taken great pains to consult as many of the subscribers as possible on any necessary changes. He could not resist pointing out the many expenses involved in running the concerts, the cost of which had increased; he had, he said, absorbed the increase without putting up the cost of tickets (though he conveniently ignored the increase of the previous year).

He ended on a defiant note, writing: 'The concerts in Newcastle have always been submitted to the Convenience and Pleasure of the Subscribers; As such I have some Reasons to believe they have hitherto been approved; and I hope they will continue as such, while I have the honour to conduct them.'

This confident tone was, in part at least, assumed. Another letter, sent to the *Journal* four months later, in March 1759, suggests that Avison had reached a very low point and a crisis of confidence. This second letter was signed Marcellinus, and was probably written by John Garth (who was in the throes of arranging the psalms of Marcello at this time).[87] Marcellinus/Garth remarked that 'our conductor has lately been called to account for assuming the sole direction of both the performance and subscription, and thereby giving offence where he intended a service'. Avison's assumption of both these roles had, of course, occurred 20 years previously, under circumstances where it looked as if the series would collapse completely; it was clearly owing to him that the series had survived, although it seems that this had been largely forgotten. The criticism had plainly been extensive, and had unsettled and distressed him; Marcellinus claimed that he had decided to give up the financial management of the series 'to any gentleman who would undertake it' and would submit to their orders 'rather chusing to assist than preside where it was so precarious to please'. Avison had clearly come to a point where he felt it was impossible to please his critics.

No gentleman seems to have come forward to take on the management of the series. Perhaps it was borne in on Avison's critics just how onerous the task was, or perhaps his threat to bow out alarmed subscribers into a realisation of how much they owed to him. In any event, he was persuaded to carry on as before. Some residual opposition may have persisted; Marcellinus devoted a substantial part of his letter to pointing out how lucky Newcastle was to have Avison, listing the jobs in London, York, Dublin and Edinburgh which he claimed Avison had turned down in favour of remaining at home in Newcastle.

Portrait of a musician

'The only way to perpetuate Music'
Newcastle Journal December 20-27, 1760

In the middle of all the unpleasant wrangling and dispiriting arguments came a piece of welcome good news. In 1759, Avison's elder brother, Edward – who was in his mid-50s – married. His wife was Ann Kell, a 36-year-old widow whose first marriage had been into a family of Newcastle waits familiar to the Avisons. Ann may have been well-off even before her marriage to Edward, who was himself by this time a wealthy man; the new Mrs Avison was already known for her charitable giving.

One of Ann's favoured charities was founded in October 1760. The Lying-In Hospital in Rosemary Lane (just doors away from Avison's and Catherine's home) was set up to provide free midwifery care for poor women, with the support of qualified medical staff; it was funded by public subscription and was particularly intended to help the wives of soldiers and seamen whose husbands might be absent in the service of the nation – a patriotic gesture in a time of war. Although it was managed by men, an all-female committee was formed from regular subscribers to the charity to visit the women being cared for and to ensure that the hospital was being properly run. Edward's new wife Ann contributed five guineas annually to the hospital and was one of the 12-strong women's committee, together with the wives of gentry and professional men, and the occasional single lady. Ann also subscribed, as did Avison, to a book published in aid of the hospital – Jane Gomeldon's *The Medley, Consisting of Thirty-One Essays, on Various Subjects*.[88]

The charity was one apparently dear to the entire family; in April 1761 Avison held a benefit concert for the hospital, raising £19 for the cause. The fact that this was about half the amount his concert for the Infirmary had raised a decade earlier may reflect on the financial situation of the war years rather than the popularity of the charity. Catherine shortly afterwards joined her sister-in-law on the ladies' committee and continued as a visitor to the hospital until her death.

Professionally, Avison's position continued to be a little shaky for two or three years. Charles Claget apparently succeeded in convincing Avison and his supporters that his intentions were benign and lingered in the town, holding another benefit in April 1759 with the help of several performers from Durham Cathedral. By June, he had been joined by his younger brother, Walter, a cellist and flute player, and the brothers held a concert in June 1759.

Newspaper advertisements for this concert include the first-known programme for any concert held in Newcastle. The concert started with an overture by Handel, continued with an unidentified song, then a flute concerto played, and probably composed, by Walter. After another song, the first act of the concert concluded with a concerto grosso by Sammartini. In the second act, a Geminiani concerto was followed by a cello solo from Walter, a song and a duet, then a violin solo by Signor Pietro Nardini, an Italian violinist who had been a pupil of Tartini; it is not clear whether Nardini himself played in the concert or whether one of the Claget brothers played his composition – the latter is probably more likely. The concert ended with a piece for full orchestra including the novelty of French horns and kettle drums, neither of which were heard very often in Newcastle. The Clagets also entertained the audience with music during the interval, playing Scots tunes on violin, cello and flute.

The Claget brothers do not seem to have held an Assize Week concert to compete with Avison's concert at which Felice Giardini was a guest performer. The fact that the Clagets let pass such a good opportunity for earning money suggests that they had either come to an agreement with Avison, or were treading carefully and being diplomatic. They put on another concert in September, however, barely a week before the subscription series began; this concert included works by Corelli on the 'Angelick Organ', an instrument, the advertisement claimed, 'admired by the greatest Judges for its Delicacy and Sweetness, superior to all others'. This new instrument may have been one of Charles Claget's inventions, for throughout his life he regularly produced novelties of this kind; new instruments exercised a fascination on audiences. Few survived, and the 'Angelick Organ' was not one of those that did.

Avison's advertisement for the winter subscription series displayed an unusual lack of confidence. His advertisements were usually bold and spare statements of place, price and dates but the paragraphs that appeared in local papers for a month from the end of August 1759 were softened and tempered by diplomatic phrases, clearly intended to reassure subscribers that he was not acting in a despotic manner and was open to comments. He started by remarking that 'I take the Liberty to offer to you by this early Application my Proposals for the winter concerts' – the word proposals suggests a certain provisionality which might be amenable to change, particularly as he had put forward the suggestions early, presumably to allow plenty of time for changes if required. He did indeed make a slight alteration to the later versions of the advertisement to make the vexed question of transferral of tickets clear but missed the deadline for inclusion in the papers and had to wait an extra week for the changes to appear.

After his initial polite phrases, Avison then went on to stress his willingness to listen to the wishes of his subscribers, adding that 'the Favour of your Commands any Time before the Opening of the Concerts on the first Thursday in October, will be gratefully acknowledged'. He ended by describing himself, with the elaborate formality of the period, but with, for Avison, unusual humility, as 'Your obliged, and most obedient humble servant'. He also took care to lay out ticket conditions in full, to avoid any later claim that they had not been made clear.

One thing he did not stress, however, was a rise in the cost of the subscription by two shillings, from 13 shillings to 15. Apparently, income was still not keeping up with expenditure. This difficulty was clearly universal throughout the region for at about this time John Garth's series in Durham finally ceased. Garth made peace with the Cathedral personnel and for a number of years collaborated with them in running mid-year concerts, although he does not seem any longer to have been involved in the winter series. The situation was also eased by the death of James Hesletine in 1763; his successor was a younger and more diplomatic man. Avison had, it seems, already withdrawn from involvement in the Durham series; he and Garth remained friends, however, and Garth continued to play in Newcastle concerts.

As far as the Clagets were concerned, it transpired that Avison had nothing long-term to fear from them. The younger brother, Walter, had never intended to stay more than a month or two and moved on to Edinburgh in the middle of 1759. Charles Claget lingered a little longer, attaching himself to the theatre company when it returned for its winter season; he appeared in a pantomine as its chief character, Harlequin, a non-speaking, non-singing part whose spectacular acrobatics and 'transformations' were the centrepiece of the action.

But he held no more concerts and did not advertise his school again; by the end of the year he had followed his brother to Edinburgh.

The conditions for the winter series apparently satisfied the subscribers and the series seems to have proceeded without incident. One of the rare reviews of Avison's concerts appeared in the *Newcastle Journal* of 1759 and shows that he had clearly been persuaded by the continuing serious political situation to give the repertoire performed a distinct patriotic slant. 'At Mr Avison's Concert,' wrote the *Journal*'s correspondent, 'were perform'd several excellent Pieces of Music, suitable to the Occasion; and each Act was opened with Songs such as Britons-strike-home, Rule Britannia, God save the King, &c. The Songs were several Times encored, and the Company, at the close of the Concert expressed their high Approbation of the Whole by three Huzzas.'

After all this furore, 1760 was a quiet year, notable for three events – two deaths and a visit from an old friend. Throughout August and September, Avison's friend and patron, George Bowes of Gibside, was intermittently ill and frequently in the care of his doctor; on September 17 he died at the age of only 59.[89] Although his wife and daughter continued to support musicians and to subscribe to new publications, the summer parties at Gibside seem to have ceased. Avison must have felt the loss of the money he had received for his summer visits and for teaching the young Miss Bowes, but he had made good friends through the connection, including Felice Giardini.

The second death was that of the King, George II, on October 25, 1760. Respect and courtesy demanded the immediate suspension of all public entertainments, including the subscription series; the suspension was short-lived, however, and the series resumed in late November.

If these events were sombre occasions, the third notable occurrence of the winter was much more palatable – a visit from the musician Avison respected above all others, Francesco Geminiani.

Since their first encounter, Avison and his old teacher had led radically different lives. Avison had returned to his native town and stayed there; although he clearly travelled much about the North East in his daily work, and occasionally further (his visit to Cambridge in 1755 to visit Thomas Gray, for instance), he had confined himself to a relatively small portion of the world. Geminiani, on the other hand, had become restless, travelling frequently between London, Paris and Dublin; he kept himself busy with composition, with printing editions of his works, with concerts and with operas although he never again achieved the level of success that had been his when he first met Avison in the 1730s.

In December 1760, Geminiani came to visit his old pupil; he was apparently travelling between Edinburgh and London, and paused to stay a few days with the Avisons in Rosemary Lane. The visit was known to music-lovers; at least one hastened to pay his compliments to the composer and later wrote anonymously to the *Newcastle Journal* to express his admiration. The writer was obviously inclined to make an uncritical and adulatory view of the revered master, writing 'I cannot describe the Satisfaction I felt in observing this Illustrious Artist … possessed of all his Faculties, and of so lively an Imagination to keep up an entertaining Conversation for several Hours together.' The writer overestimated Geminiani's age, suggesting that he was 88 when in fact he was around 75; perhaps the composer looked older than his years.

Conversation was not the only entertainment on offer and it was hardly surprising that the talk turned to music. Whether Avison or Geminiani played is not recorded, but Avison's elder surviving son, Edward, then aged 13, played one or two pieces on the harpsichord. Geminiani was delighted and inclined to be sentimental. The writer to the *Journal* records that 'he took [Edward] in his Arms with an Earnestness, which affected them both', saying to Avison: 'My Friend, I love all your Productions. You are my Heir. This boy will be yours. Take care of him. To raise up Geniuses like him is the only way to perpetuate Music.'

The anonymous writer was clearly one of Avison's keen supporters as he ended: 'I send this little Anecdote … as it does Honour to our Organist, and is a recent Proof of the Fame of his Music.'

But Geminiani had already discovered that fame was fleeting and that public taste changed rapidly. It was to be a lesson that Avison learned too. The first signs of it can be seen in the music that his friend John Garth was composing in Durham – Garth's cello concertos that pitted a virtuoso solo instrument against an orchestra were very different from Avison's concerti grossi, where soloists briefly rose out of the general texture, then faded back into it. The Italian style, championed by Geminiani and Avison, and the concerto grosso, were becoming old-fashioned.

~

It was at this point that Avison chose to have his portrait painted.

The portrait, which is now the property of St Nicholas' Cathedral, has the name F. Lindo and the date 1761 on the backing board.[90] Francis Lindo was a portrait painter in crayons and oils and most of his work seems to have been done in lowland Scotland, and Aberdeenshire; however, he painted a portrait of Hugh Percy, later the second Duke of Northumberland in 1765.[91] Little is known of his life and there is no hint of why Avison chose him as the artist.

The portrait is not of Lindo's best and it has been suggested that the painting that survives is in fact a copy of the original, possibly done by one of Avison's amateur artist friends. The artist has made Avison look rather younger than his 50 years but flattering portraits are not unusual. Avison is informally dressed, wearing his own hair tied back by a black ribbon, rather than a wig;[92] he holds a sheet of music and looks off into the visionary distance, as if looking to the future – perhaps the artist was trying to suggest that Charles Avison's name and music would last for many years to come.

'Dull songs and sleepy airs'

'In the Manner of Ranelagh Gardens in London'
Newcastle Courant July 4, 1761

The early 1760s were notable for the appearance in Newcastle of a new type of concert, of which Avison disapproved heartily. In June 1761, celebrations were held in the town to mark the birthday of the Prince of Wales who, only four months later, was to become King George III. Amongst the celebrations was a 'Grand Concert of Musick', held not by Avison in the Assembly Rooms, but outdoors in pleasure gardens just outside the town walls.[93]

Pleasure gardens had been popular in London for most of the century but the fashion had been slow in reaching the North East, perhaps because of fears about the weather. During the 1750s, the Durham Cathedral choir had held several concerts at Old Durham, a house just outside the city, where ladies and gentlemen enjoyed a walk in fine weather but these were isolated concerts obviously regarded as a novelty and never became regular events, as in the pleasure gardens of London.

The venue for the celebratory concert on June 4, 1760, was 'Mr Callender's new Ranelaugh Gardens'. The Callenders were a family of local seedsmen whose nursery gardens lay outside the town walls (opposite the modern-day football stadium);[94] they seem to have decided to cash in on their property by opening it to ladies and gentlemen who wished for a pleasant stroll, providing music in the style of the London Gardens. They even went so far as to name the gardens for one of the best-known London venues.

The gardens may have been used for this purpose for some years previously, for the advertisement for the celebratory concert refers to 'the Opening for the Season' suggesting that the concert was neither an isolated event nor a new one. If the gardens had been operating as an entertainment venue for two or three years, then Avison's summer series of concerts, which lasted a mere three years between 1757 and 1759, may have been a deliberate attempt to present a rival entertainment.

Avison disliked the idea of garden concerts intensely. The emphasis in the London gardens was on entertainment, with the music tending to be a mere background to strolls, chatting with friends and partaking of supper. As a result, much of the music performed in the gardens was vocal music – songs, short cantatas and other slight pieces often performed by attractive and engaging young actresses. Avison castigated the gardens for producing 'a flood of nonsense' in the form of 'shallow and unconnected Compositions' and seems to have decided to have nothing to do with the Newcastle enterprise.[95] He clearly felt that this was one downside of the new commercialisation: a pandering to popular taste with little regard for the quality of the music .

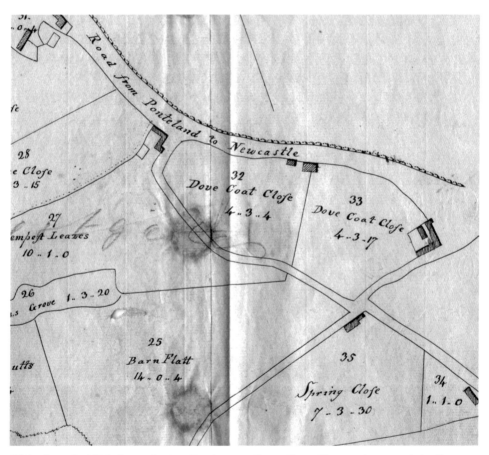

This plan of c1802 shows Spring Gardens, or Dove Coat Close as it was originally known, just to the south of what is now Barrack Road.

The Callenders' garden, later renamed Spring Gardens after another London venue, seems to have been rather ad hoc to begin with, but a house for the musicians was certainly built by 1761 – this probably looked like a summerhouse or elaborate bandstand. Refreshments were also available, and a tea house was built around 1763 or 1764. The band was made up of the usual local musicians (local professional players were so few in number that they all appeared in all bands) and the singers were chiefly actresses from the local theatre company, with an occasional actor or singing man from Durham Cathedral.

Avison's decision to remain aloof from the gardens did not mean that his music was not played there; on August 6, 1760, for instance, a march he had composed for the Yorkshire Buffs Regiment was played. (This had been written for the Colonel of the militia regiment, John Grimston of Kilnwick in Yorkshire, who later subscribed to Avison's publications.[96]) Nevertheless, Avison certainly had extensive contacts with the performers; not only were the members of the band also members of his own concert band, but he had become acquainted with the musical director of the garden concerts, a young and ambitious German musician called William Herschel. Herschel would later become better known as an astronomer.

Herschel was a Hanoverian by birth and, with his brother Jacob, had been attracted to London by accounts of the money that could be made there.[97] The Herschel brothers soon realised that all the big opportunities were enjoyed by Italian musicians and that their own chances of success were limited. Jacob cut his losses and went back to Hanover, but William joined the band of a regiment raised by the Earl of Darlington and travelled north with it to its quarters at Richmond in Yorkshire. The job offered the security of a reasonable salary but the new life was no more congenial to him than the old and he left after only a short while to set himself up as a music teacher in Sunderland.

Sunderland was a thriving port, midway in size between Newcastle and Durham, and Herschel evidently found the merchants anxious for improvement, for entertainment and for accomplishments for their children. He soon was much in demand, not only as a teacher, but also as a violinist and musical director. Before long, he was enjoying the positions of director of the Spring Gardens concerts and of leader of Avison's subscription concerts in Newcastle. He looked on both jobs as an opportunity to get his compositions played more frequently, although the constant travelling on horseback, in all weathers, between Newcastle and Sunderland seems to have wearied him.

Herschel was quickly assimilated into the musical life of the area and became very friendly with Avison and with John Garth; in August 1761, Sir Ralph and Lady Milbanke invited all three men to Halnaby in Yorkshire, to meet the Duke of York, brother of George III and a man very musically inclined; he played the cello very well and Avison, Herschel and Garth were invited to accompany him.

Avison's non-involvement in the garden concerts allowed him to find time for more composition. At long last he found time to work on one of the psalms of Benedetto Marcello,

George III was crowned King on September 22, 1761 at the age of 22.

which took final shape as *The King shall be joyful in thy Strength,* performed on the day of George III's coronation, September 22, 1761. The music has unfortunately been lost but the words were printed in local papers and show that the anthem included solos, duets and choruses. On Coronation Day the concert at which the anthem was performed was part of extensive celebrations including the ringing of bells, speeches, volleys of gunfire, an Assembly and the replacement of water in the fountain on the Sandhill with wine.

1761 was notable for the appointment of Avison's old friend, John Brown, as vicar of St Nicholas' church; the two men had very similar views on church music and a joint interest in painting and literature, and were to work well together for several years. But 1762 was more sombre, bringing the sad news of

Geminiani's death in Dublin, although Avison could not bring himself to pen an obituary for his old master until six years later.

Otherwise, the year was very quiet, proceeding much as usual, although Avison scored a notable triumph in October when he engaged the services of a well-known Italian singer for one of the subscription concerts. Signora Clementina Cremonini had been engaged direct from Italy by the Edinburgh Musical Society who wanted her to sing in their concerts; they were prepared only to accept the best singers and paid her travel expenses to Scotland. Clementina Cremonini, however, was not satisfied with the salary they offered and almost immediately absconded to London in search of a better offer; Avison intercepted her as she travelled south. There is no record of what she sang in the subscription concert but she clearly enthralled the audience; one gentleman was moved to write poetry in her praise, and sent the result to the *Newcastle Courant*. The opening lines convey his delight in a singer he compared with the angels:

> *When Cremonini sings she thrills my Soul*
> *With heavenly Sounds, whose Powers controul*
> *Each turbulent Passion, and inspires*
> *My much transported Heart with soft Desires.*[98]

The Spring Gardens concerts continued to thrive in 1763; in price they were competitive with Avison's subscription series, offering a season ticket for half a guinea – the same price as the subscription ticket for Avison's concerts, but the Spring Gardens season offered four more concerts for the money. It was the price of individual tickets which was significant, however. Music-lovers paid three shillings for one of Avison's concerts but only one shilling for a night in the gardens, where more was on offer than just music. The cheaper price meant that the garden concerts were affordable to a much wider section of the population, including less well-educated members of society. This may have been one of Avison's objections to garden concerts; in the *Essay on Musical Expression* he had maintained that good taste in all the arts was dependent on good education – only available to those who could afford to pay for it.

If Avison disliked the garden concerts, it can only be imagined how he reacted to a visitor to Newcastle in the summer of 1763. Mr Lambourn 'MUSICIAN of London and late of the KING'S THEATRE, in the Hay-Market' offered a series of performances on the musical glasses. For those who wanted to hear him play he was available between 9 and 12 every morning at his lodgings in the Black-Bull and Post-Boy. One of his advertisements confidently claimed that the musical glasses were 'beyond any conception to those who have not heard them'.[99]

Much more to Avison's taste would probably have been the Italian musicians who called in at Newcastle on their way from Edinburgh to London in September 1763. They offered to treat music-lovers in Newcastle (described in their advertisements as 'this opulent town') to an opera by Pergolesi called *The Maid, the Mistress*. It is not clear whether they sang in Italian or English; copies of the libretto had both Italian and English words.

Avison clearly liked Pergolesi's music, although he was not uncritical of it; in his *Essay*, he had written that Pergolesi's harmony was at times extreme and unnatural but that this fault was often possible to ignore. 'The frequent Delicacy of whose Airs is so striking, that we almost forget the Defect of Harmony under which they often labour. Their faults are lost amidst their Excellencies; and the Critic of Taste is almost tempted to blame his own Severity in censoring Compositions in which he finds Charms so powerful and commanding.[100] It is entirely possible that Avison was in the audience applauding *The Maid, the Mistress*.

During these relatively quiet years, Avison seems to have concentrated on producing more works of his own. Opus 7 had been published in 1760; Opus 8, dedicated to Mary Eleanor Bowes, the daughter of his old patron, George Bowes, appeared in 1764. Both were sonatas of the same type as Opus 5, where the harpsichord part was written out in full. He was, however, also working on something more unusual – in terms of his own output at least: he was writing an oratorio. Avison had never produced a great deal of vocal music compared to the amount of instrumental music he wrote and very little was published; this was despite the view generally held in the 18th century that vocal music was superior to instrumental, because of its ability to better express emotions.[101]

The oratorio was both a favour for his good friend, Felice Giardini, and a philanthropic gesture, for it was intended as a fundraiser for the Lock Hospital in London, much as Handel's oratorios raised money for the Foundling Hospital.[102] Giardini conceived of setting a story which had not previously appeared in music, that of Ruth from the Old Testament, but apparently did not wish to compose all the music himself. A story that he originally asked

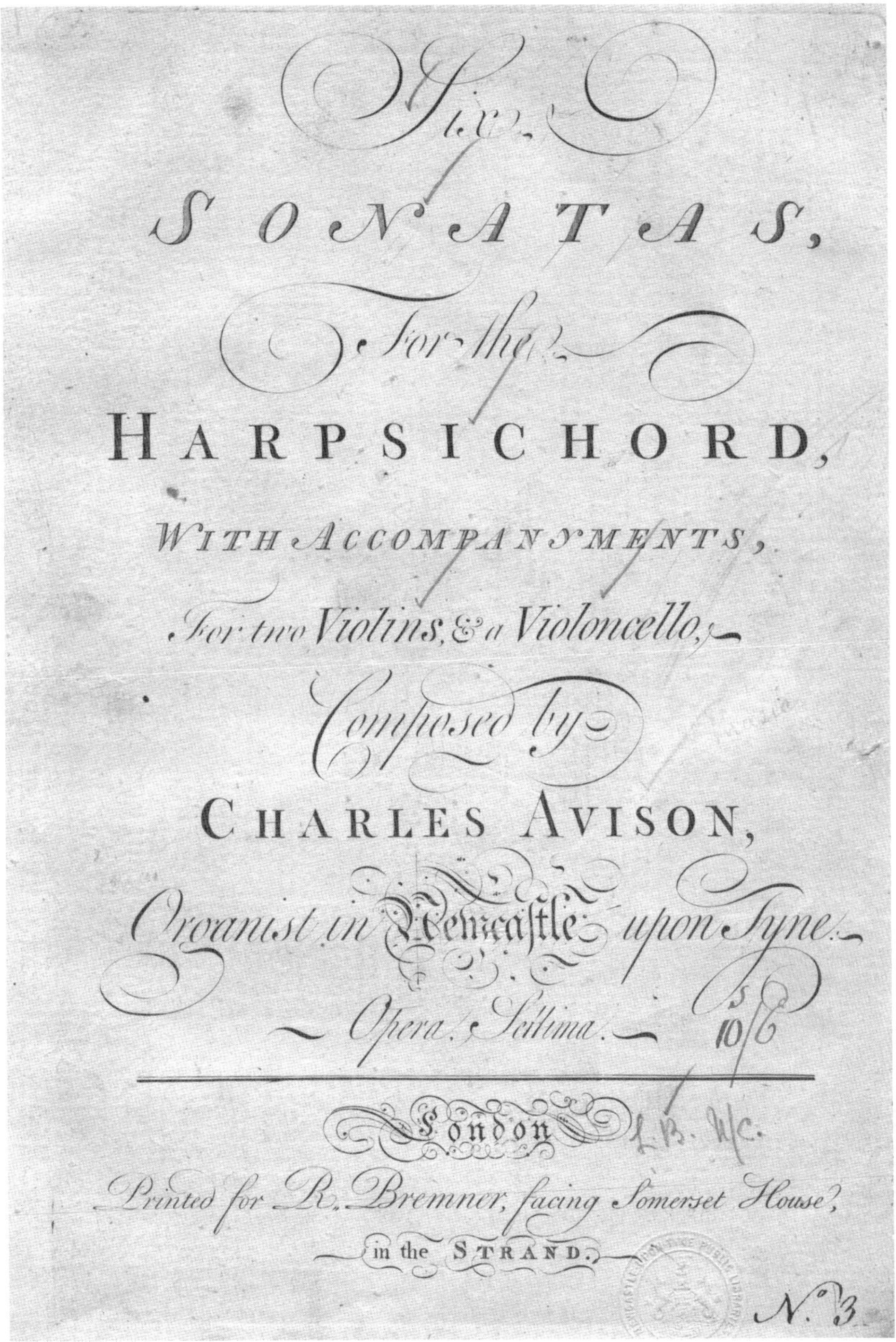

Six

SONATAS,

For the

HARPSICHORD,

WITH ACCOMPANYMENTS,

For two *Violins*, & a *Violoncello*,

Composed by

CHARLES AVISON,

Organist in Newcastle upon Tyne.

~ *Opera Settima.* ~ 10/6

London   L.B. W.C.

Printed for R. Bremner, facing Somerset House,

in the STRAND.

N.º 3

Avison to write the first act, and William Boyce the third, providing the second act himself, may be apocryphal; at the first performance on February 13, 1765, Avison provided the music for both the outer acts. He may well have been present for the performance; it is difficult to believe that he would willingly have missed such an event.

The production of an oratorio was in itself an unusual enterprise at the time; Handel had established himself so firmly in charge of the genre that few other composers thought it worth their while to attempt it. *Ruth* seems to have been relatively popular; one visitor recorded herself 'much pleased with the music yesterday at the Lock Hospital[.] Avison's chorus were very fine.'[103] The work received many performances over the next few years in aid of the Lock Hospital but Avison's music was not heard after the first performance. With some brutality, Giardini abandoned the parts written by Avison and substituted music of his own. It is not clear what damage this did to the two men's friendship.

In the early 1760s, Avison was still doing well financially, despite struggles with the viability of the subscription series; sometime in 1763, he and Catherine moved to an even better house, in Green Court. This was a select square with good, roomy modern houses; the square may have been built by William Newton, the well-known local architect, who owned and lived in one of the houses. The new house had two reception rooms, called the best parlour and the red room, as well as several bedrooms; each of the reception rooms had a harpsichord. There were a number of writing desks, and the house was well-furnished with Avison's collection of books and music.[104]

The couple's three surviving children seem still to have been living at home; Jane was now 19, Edward 17 and Charles 14. As the boys matured, Avison was certainly tutoring them in music, as the anecdote about Geminiani's visit shows; eventually, Edward began to act as deputy as organist of St Nicholas' church, and Charles junior as deputy at St John's; this sort of arrangement may have been in Avison's mind when he offered to help renovate St John's organ in the late 1740s on condition he received the appointment as organist.

His financial situation continued to be excellent. His investments clearly accounted for a large part of his annual income, to the extent that in the mid-1760s, like his father before him, he felt it appropriate to term himself 'gentleman'. But this claim seems to have attracted a personal attack on himself and his family which caused him great distress. The attack came in a verse pamphlet called *The Will of a Certain Northern Vicar* which purported to be the will of the Vicar of Bedlington, John Ellison, who was also lecturer at St Andrew's church in Newcastle. He was not the author of the poem, however, but one of its victims.[105]

In the Will, Ellison is said to leave legacies which match the foibles and vices of the objects of his satire. Many local notables were satirised in the pamphlet but the verse about Avison's family seems to have been particularly vicious, and was followed up by an even nastier pamphlet.[106] Avison's musical gifts were described as 'sniv'ling talents', his music as 'dull songs and sleepy airs'. Catherine was described as dissimulating and affected, with a 'sland'rous tongue, with venom swell'd'. The three children were allegedly badly educated; they were all described as 'low-bred wretches'.

Avison appears to have been unable to allow criticism to pass, as his swift and sharp response to Hayes's comments about the *Essay* had demonstrated. His first reaction was to write to the local papers. The advertisement that appeared in the *Newcastle Chronicle* on September 14, 1765 was not a reasoned response – Avison claimed that he knew the identity of the author, that it was a Yorkshire clergyman and that the kindest thing would be to take him to the Bedlam mad-house at once. He was, Avison claimed, 'shatter-brain'd' and had 'taken it into his crazy pate, to imagine that he has been

The Vicar dictates his will to his lawyer, from The Will of a Certain Northern Vicar.

excessively witty'. This did not however sufficiently relieve Avison's feelings, and he soon retaliated with a poem of his own in which he named the 'certain Northern Vicar' as the Revd William Cooper, Rector of Kirby Wiske in Yorkshire.[107]

It is hard to believe that Avison took the step of naming his alleged attacker without at least some evidence but he seems to have miscalculated. Cooper at once publicly denied the accusation although many people chose not to believe the denial.[108] A supporter of Cooper wrote a pamphlet, accusing Avison of making wild accusations fuelled by coffee-house gossip.

The dispute, never fully resolved, marred what might otherwise have been a moment for celebration: the 30th anniversary of Avison's management of the subscription series (although the calculation did not take account of the fact that his control had been strictly unofficial for the first three years). Avison had already courted controversy over this anniversary season, for he had again raised the cost of subscription. He had not acted lightly, and had taken the precaution of consulting a good number of the subscribers before putting forward his plans for an increase in the annual subscription from 15 shillings to one guinea – a hefty increase of over 25%. He tempered the blow by offering an extra two concerts: 14 rather than 12.

Avison had not consulted enough people; immediate objections were made by some loyal subscribers. 'The plan,' Avison wrote in a second advertisement to the papers, 'is objected to by some, who have hitherto honoured him with their Favours'. He was willing, he said, 'as far as is within his Power, to make it agreeable to all his Friends'. He altered the terms of subscription again, attempting to save at least part of the planned increase in income. The result was a compromise awkward in the extreme: those who objected to the increase could pay the old rate and obtain admission to the usual 12 concerts; those who did not object could pay the higher price and attend 14 concerts. If insufficient people chose the latter option, there would not be sufficient funds to run two extra concerts, in which case they would be cancelled and the extra contributions refunded.

Surprisingly, the compromise seems to have worked – the same alternatives were offered by the series in 1766.

By then, however, Avison's world had changed considerably. If 1765 had been a trying year, 1766 was to prove much worse.

Tragedies

'Much regretted by ... Friends and Acquaintances'
Newcastle Courant October 16, 1766

The years from 1766 were quiet years for Avison from a professional point of view. The Spring Gardens concerts ceased, apparently hastened by a year of bad weather; Darlington music-lovers copied his idea for a summer series of concerts. In Durham, John Garth was abandoning concert promotion to concentrate on teaching; he still regularly made the trip to Newcastle to play in Avison's concerts, however. The round of mid-year and subscription concerts continued as usual with an occasional variation as in February 1766, when Avison held a concert in honour of the Queen's birthday. Subscribers seem to have embraced the idea of a two-tier subscription series, with a choice of 12 or 14 concerts.

On a personal level, however, the years between 1766 and 1770 were difficult and traumatic, deeply depressing. 1766 saw the deaths of two of the people to whom he was closest.

John Brown, whom he had originally met through the musical society at Gilpin's house in Carlisle, had remained a close friend. Since he had been inducted as Vicar of St Nicholas, in 1761, he and Avison had worked together extremely well. They held very similar views on church music and co-operated to make music at St Nicholas' simple, austere and, above all, dedicated to the service of piety and devotion. Both believed that music was in the service of religion, not an end in itself; as Avison had written in his *Essay*, 'we seem at present almost to have forgot that Devotion is the

Dr. Brown.

original and proper End of it'.

They also shared the idea that vocal music should be based on the ideas of the ancient Greeks, because, as Avison had said, of 'the pure Simplicity of its Melody'. Brown's views were more dogmatic than Avison's, however, and rather less practical. He approached music from a doctrinal and theological standpoint and laid out his views in detail in his own book on music with the lengthy title of *A Dissertation on the Rise, Union, and Power, the Progressions, Separations, and Corruptions, of Poetry and Music* published in 1763.

To Brown, music could not be separated from poetry and, above all, from a moral purpose. Music had a duty to serve religion, truth, justice and morals, and should never be used for anything so trivial as amusement. He disapproved of instrumental music, which could not explicitly convey any moral lessons, and championed vocal music, which could, through its words. Opera was far too frivolous for him, and oratorio savoured too much of the melodramatic and trivial, although he greatly admired Handel. He reconciled himself to the dilemma this caused by blaming the faults of oratorio on librettists and even wrote a libretto for an oratorio, *The Cure of Saul*, to show how it should be done; this was later set to music by Samuel Arnold. Avison did not go so far in condemning instrumental music – he had, after all, devoted a great deal of his life to giving people pleasure with it. Any disagreement over these points, however, does not seem to have spoiled the friendship between the two men;

A 19th-century drawing of Newcastle vicarage, home of John Brown.

From the collections of Literary & Philosophical Society, Newcastle

Derwentwater, painted by William Gilpin.

Brown held regular Sunday evening musical gatherings in a room especially built onto the vicarage for the purpose and Avison was a regular and valued attender.

They shared views on many other topics, on painting for instance, and literature. Brown was one of the earliest authors on landscape and picturesque beauty and made an annual visit to Keswick, describing what he saw in a famous letter published in 1766.[109] Avison accompanied him on at least one of these visits, together with William Gilpin, who described how they chanced upon a view of Derwentwater; Avison was evidently entranced and exclaimed, 'Here is beauty indeed – beauty lying in the lap of Horrour!'[110] This sense of awe, of majestic and sublime wildness, verging on a pleasurable shudder of fear, epitomised the Lake District and other mountainous regions in the eyes of 18th-century travellers.

Brown may have helped to spread knowledge of Avison's work in Europe through his wide literary contacts. His own reputation as a writer had begun in 1745 with the publication of *An Essay on Satire*; later work brought him into contact with Matthieu Maty, founder of the *Journal Britannique* which introduced British publications to the rest of Europe by means of reviews and extracts. Maty gave a favourable review to Brown's *Essays on the Characteristics of the Earl of Shaftesbury* in 1751,[111] and invited him to a weekly tea-club; one of the other members was the Reverend John Jortin, whose thoughts on the music of the ancient world were published by Avison in the second edition of the *Essay on Musical Expression* in 1753. Avison may have lived outside the hub of activity that was London, but he was far from isolated and was in correspondence with many of the main thinkers in the period. In the meantime, Brown did him a favour and used Maty's *Journal Britannique* for a long and favourable review of the *Essay on Musical Expression*.[112]

Relations were less cordial, however, between Brown and another friend of Avison's, William Mason, precentor of York Minster and an amateur composer himself. (see page 50) Mason was a man prone to a sharp wit and in the mid-1760s he exercised that wit on John Brown, penning a poem satirising Brown and his ideas. The poem distressed Brown, and Avison on his behalf (no doubt the poem written by the 'northern vicar' still preyed on Avison's mind). But no one seems to have anticipated what might ensue. Brown had always been subject to bouts of deep and prolonged depression; in the throes of such a fit, he committed suicide in 1766.

In the aftermath of Brown's death, Mason was struck by guilt, convinced that his poem must have precipitated Brown's death; his friends assured him that it had not, but he could never quite convince himself. Brown had made his will, listing Avison amongst his 'esteemed friends' and leaving him a mourning ring.

~

On Wednesday October 15, 1766, Avison was struck by an even more traumatic event – the death of his wife, just one week after the start of the new season's subscription concerts. Catherine was 53 years old and had been ill for some time with 'a lingering illness which she bore with great resignation';[113] her illness was probably tuberculosis which was often described in this way. She was buried in St Andrew's churchyard, near the main entrance to the church.

~

Under the circumstances, it is not surprising that Avison turned to the occupation that had always engrossed and consoled him – composition. He was in the middle of preparing a set of new concertos for his concert band and published this Opus 9 in two sets of six, in 1766 and 1767. Such was his state of mind that he commented in the preface that the concertos would probably be the last he ever published. He also showed a rather depressed awareness that his style of writing was now a trifle dated, commenting that he had 'endeavoured to avoid the rapid Style of Composition now in vogue'.[114] This style he thought turgid and bombastic and 'to suit very ill with the native Charms of Melody, but still worse with the nobler Powers of Harmony'.

He did, however, publish one more set of concertos, Opus 10, in 1769 – perhaps the needs of his concert band dictated that he continued to compose, or perhaps he found it a solace in moments of grief and depression. In addition, he may have been working on arrangements of music by the Italian composer, Carlo Clari; Clari's madrigals were very popular and Avison adapted some of them by substituting texts from the Bible for the original secular texts.[115] In his preface he commented that: 'To consecrate the powers of Music to Service of religion is a national service, as it answers the noblest purpose for which music was originally intended.' This was a sentiment that his old friend Dr Brown would have wholeheartedly supported. The surviving manuscript, in Newcastle City Library, is patently a neat copy intended for the publisher (see colour section pages 6-7) but the works were never published; perhaps this was a project Avison had in progress at the time of his death.[116]

He seems to have descended into a quiet contemplative melancholy. In 1768, his thoughts were still on the death of friends; he at last penned and published a tribute to his old teacher, Geminiani, sending it to the *Newcastle Courant* under the initials C.A. In it he outlined the career of 'this celebrated musician' and praised his character and abilities, calling him an 'extraordinary man' finishing by summarising what was, for Avison, the crux of Geminiani's thinking and understanding. 'I … revere his Memory in this very Expression which I have often heard him repeat, – That Truth and Simplicity are the best Criterion of the fine Arts, as they are of the good Conduct in human Life.'

Even more poignant was the brief note that Avison sent to another local publication, the *Literary Register*, in 1769, written 'on viewing a portrait of the celebrated GEMINIANI'. Avison's melancholy and his disillusion with the contemporary style of music, and his concern over political events at home and abroad came through very clearly in these few words; he could, however, still find a faint suggestion of hope for the future. 'While contending nations alarm the world abroad, and interiour commotions at home, I peruse thy pacific page, and wonder where the powers of music are fled, not to harmonise the passions of men; yet still the dulcet strains will live in congenial souls, to smooth the path of life which providence has given to lovers of harmony.'[117]

During these years, Avison also meditated on the decline of patronage, regretting that more men and women were not coming forward to assist men of learning and promise. He wrote to the *Literary Register*: 'How much might be expected in public life were not the ministers of government and the affluent, more attached to their ambition and pleasure, than the assisting of men of genius and worth, deserving their protection'.[118] Perhaps he was thinking of George Bowes, William Ord, Ralph Milbanke and Walter Blackett, and others, who had helped his own career over the years. But times were changing; the old patronage system which had supported musicians for centuries was irrevocably breaking down under commercial pressures. Avison and other musicians now depended not so much on the support of a rich patron but on the more fickle tastes of a wider public, attending concerts and buying his music and his service as a teacher. Avison plainly saw this and had spent his working life exploiting the possibilities but still regretted the passing of the old ways.

In the last years of his life, he found comfort in reading, both words and music, turning to old favourites like Geminiani and Lawrence Sterne, whose *Tristram Shandy* was a constant companion. He put many of his ideas into print at this time, penning short paragraphs for the *Literary Register* under the initials C.A. and A.C.;[119] he several times sent the *Register* sections of *Tristram Shandy*, evidently pleasing young ladies of his acquaintance who were not allowed to read the entire book because of parts that were considered improper. He sent extracts from historical works – about the Court of James II, the Court of Flanders and the emperor Justinian; he forwarded remarks on modern music written by Jackson, the organist of Exeter Cathedral, remarks that he called 'judicious, critical and just'. Extracts from plays and anecdotes taken from old books, stories about generosity from his own experience and articles about bishops were all considered by Avison as worthy of general notice.

Many of the extracts were no doubt taken from books in his own possession; he is known to have subscribed to a number of works. Inevitably, there was much music amongst his books – he subscribed to concertos and trio sonatas by Michael Festing, songs and harpsichord suites by John Allcock, harpsichord works by James Nares (once organist of York Minster), and songs by Thomas Chilcott. Overtures by Francesco Barsanti and solos for flute, violin or oboe by Alessandro Bezozzi (a musician much liked by George Bowes and his wife) demonstrate his continuing interest in Italian music. He also bought copies of John Garth's edition of Marcello's Psalms and an Ode to the King of Prussia by one of his pupils, Matthias Hawdon, who had taken over the post of organist at Holy Trinity, Hull, after the death of Charles' brother, William.

He was also fond of poetry, subscribing to poems by Newcastle poets, Thomas Hudson and John Cunningham, and to a publication by Christopher Smart in London which features two odes – one on good-nature and the other on ill-nature. A book by Musgrave Heighington, a native of Durham and at various times organist of Holy Trinity Hull (where he had been William Avison's predecessor) and of Great Yarmouth, combined the two interests

LIST *of* SUBSCRIBERS.

Mrs Armſtrong of *Gibſide*
Mr Aviſon, Organiſt of St *Nicholas* in *Newcaſtle upon Tyne*
Mr Thomas Aubone, in the *Cloſe, Newcaſtle*
Anonymous

B

Right Hon. Earl of *Breadalbane,* 4 Copies
Right Hon. Counteſs of *Breadalbane,* 2 Copies
Sir Walter Blackett, Bart. of Wallington, Member of Parliament for *Newcaſtle upon Tyne,* 2 Copies
Mrs Bowes, of *Gibſide,* 2 Copies
Miſs Bowes, of *Gibſide,* 2 Copies
Miſs Jane Bowes of *Durham*
Thomas Bainbridge, Eſq; of *Derby*
John Baker, Eſq; of *Newcaſtle upon Tyne*
George Baker, Eſq; of *Ellimore,* 5 Copies
Mr George Baker of *Crooke*
Miſs Baker of *Crooke*
Charles Boſvile, Eſq; of *Byana,* near *Eccleſhall, Staffordſhire,* 4 Copies
Mrs Eliz. Boſvile, of *Byana,* 2 Copies
Ralph Bates, Eſq; of *Newcaſtle upon Tyne,* 2 Copies
Rev. Mr Thomas Bates, A. M. Rector of *Whalton, Northumberland*
Rev. Mr Baker, A. M. Fellow of *Brazen-noſe* Coll. *Ox.*
Mr George Barkas of *Offerton*
Mr James Barras, Merchant, in *Gateſhead*
Mr

Avison subscribed to Sixteen Discourses on several practical and important subjects by William Adey in 1760.

of poetry and music, being poetry (*Six Select Odes of Anacreon*) set to music. Sermons by Anthony Munton of Newcastle and a book by William Adey – *Sixteen Discourses on several practical and important subjects* – represented serious subjects. On a lighter note he had also subscribed to *A New general Collection of Voyages and Travels … in Europe, Asia, Africa and America* written by John Green of London. Given that he may also have purchased books on a whim or on the recommendation of friends without subscribing to them, Charles's collection of books was probably large and wide-ranging.

He also must have owned a set of the well-known journal, *The Spectator*, which he admired so much that he read it from beginning to end four times.[120]

~

On June 24, 1767, he drew up his will. The document gives a clear indication of how wealthy he had become. He refers to a deed of gift that he had just made, dividing up the stock that he owned, mainly in old South Sea Annuities, between his three children, giving his daughter Jane £800 worth of stock, and his sons Edward and Charles £100 worth each. By the terms of the will, each of the children received a harpsichord (all by excellent manufacturers) with one or two other pieces of furniture. Edward received all the other musical instruments owned by his father and the music books; Jane was given all the household goods including linen and plate. Avison's collection of books was to be divided between the three children provided they were not needed to pay any debts; surprisingly, he does not mention the portrait painted in 1761. He also recommended that as little as possible should be spent on his funeral and expressed his wish to be buried with his wife in St Andrew's churchyard.

On the night of May 9-10, 1770, Avison died, aged 61. The weather had been unseasonably bad, with surprising falls of snow, but it is not clear whether this contributed to his death, the cause of which is not known. Local papers remarked that he would be greatly missed 'for he was as much valued for the amiableness of his private character as admired for his skill in the profession, and for his excellent compositions'.[121]

Charles Avison's Will

transcript by Margaret Maddison

Newcastle June 24, 1767 having made a deed of gift of my stock of one thousand pounds in the Old South Sea Annuities, namely to my daughter Jane eight hundred pounds, to my son Edward one hundred pounds, to my son Charles one hundred pounds after my decease, I herewith add the following bequests, to my daughter Jane the double harpsicord made by Shudi, and the cabinet in her own room, to my son Edward the double harpsicord made by Kirkman and the scrutoirs* in the best parlour, to my son Charles, the double harpsicord made by Willhook and the scrutoier in the red room, All my other musical instruments and my collection of music with the plates of my concertos in score, I bequeath to my son Edward not doubting but he will make a proper use of them, my reading books may be sold if occasions should require, if not, I desire they may be divided among my children, This is my last will and testament, blessing the infinite goodness and mercy of the Almighty who has given me hopes of eternal happiness through the mediation of my saviour Jesus Christ. Charles Avison

P.S. All my household goods linnen and plate excepting the scrutoirs above mentioned, I bequeath to my daughter Jane. Charles Avison

Should my decease happen in Newcastle I desire that my remains may be laid near the south porch in Saint Andrews churchyard near the remains of my dear wife, and that the least possible expence may be laid out on my interment. Charles Avison

May every blessing attend my dear children and that they may be a comfort to theirs, as their parents have been to them.

*'scrutoir' means 'escritoire' or writing desk with compartments.

Source: The National Archives, PROB 11/360

Sons and daughters

'*Deserving the greatest Encouragement*'
Newcastle Courant January 13, 1780

Avison's death caused immediate problems for his brother Edward and his friend Robert Page, who was deputy inspector of Customs in Newcastle. Although Avison had drawn up his will in 1767, he had never had it formally witnessed. Edward and Robert made affidavits that they 'knew and were intimately acquainted with Charles Avison late of Newcastle upon Tyne in the County of Northumberland, widower, for several years standing … and also with his manner and Character of Handwriting and Subscription, having often seen him write and subscribe his name'. They declared that they had viewed the draft will, and swore to it being 'the handwriting and usual manner of subscription of him the said Charles Avison deceased'.[122]

The will was allowed and implemented.

Edward, Avison's older surviving son, took over most of his father's responsibilities. He had clearly already been acting as his father's deputy as organist of St Nicholas' church to the extent that the Corporation did not bother officially to appoint him organist but merely allowed the situation to continue. He also took on the organisation of the mid-year concerts and the winter subscription series; his first concert was held a month after the death of his father, on June 27, 1770.

Edward's first subscription series was marked by an element of controversy, although precisely what happened is not clear. One of those involved was Avison's old friend, John Garth of Durham, who had always played in Newcastle concerts; Garth was concentrating more and more on his teaching practice, and may have used the death of his old friend as a pretext for withdrawing from performing in Newcastle. Whatever the exact circumstances, Garth's behaviour (and that of some others) drew a sharp and angry response in print from an anonymous writer calling himself only Philomusicus.[123]

Philomusicus was certainly one of Avison's supporters as he had not long before written to the *Literary Register* to send them a copy of John Brown's review of the *Essay on Musical Expression* that had appeared in the *Journal Britannique*.[124]

Philomusicus rather tartly presented his compliments to 'Mr G——-H' and demanded 'if he thinks that he hath cancelled every obligation he owed to the late worthy, and ingenious Mr Avison, by playing at his concerts'. His use of the familiar 'hath' may have been intended to add to the insult; he also pointed out that Garth had been paid for playing in the concerts, implying thereby that this lessened the gesture.

It would give him 'unspeakable pleasure', Philomusicus said, if Garth, and others, had 'more harmonious and heavenly dispositions'. He described music as 'that elegant and divine Art' and ended with outspoken rancour. 'From their behaviour,' he said, 'one would imagine that it must cost them some trouble to confine their music to their heads and fingers, terribly afraid lest it should reach their hearts and humanise their selfish souls.' Garth had obviously failed to support Edward in the way that Philomusicus would have liked.

Despite this argument, Edward's career at first seemed to progress well. He continued to live at his father's house in Green Court, to teach and to play at St Nicholas. His younger brother, Charles junior, seems to have been less settled. He too had been employed as his father's deputy, at St John's church, and continued as organist there on his father's death. He seems to have occupied various lodgings about the town; in April 1771, for instance, he was lodging at 'Mr Shotton's, in the Back Row'.[125] He began to try his hand at concert promotion, holding a benefit concert for himself in April 1771, using an actress from the local theatre company as vocal soloist.

In October 1771, the advertisement for the subscription series hints at a problem, for Edward added a paragraph remarking that 'as particular care will be taken to render the Concerts worthy the Approbation of the Public, it is humbly hoped the Public will afford them their Encouragement, upon which alone the support of the entertainment depends' suggesting that support had previously been uncertain.[126] A year later more problems arose. Edward had clearly hoped to increase the profile of the concerts by hiring an up-and-coming young London singer, Miss Alphi, pupil to the celebrated castrato, Tenducci. Miss Alphi sang in the mid-year concerts in 1772 and evidently impressed audiences, but before the subscription series could begin, she eloped

Back Row, near the Castle, where Charles Avison junior lodged in 1771.

with an actor from the theatre company in Carlisle and withdrew from public performance.[127] She sent Edward a letter apologising for no longer being able to sing in his winter concerts; less than a week before the series began, Edward had to find a new singer.

He had also been forced to alter the terms of the series. On taking over, he had continued with his father's arrangement of two parallel subscriptions for 12 and 14 concerts but he had been told (or, as his advertisement put it, 'some encouragers of this entertainment had been pleased to intimate') that this arrangement was 'disagreeable'; Edward took the hint and dropped the shorter subscription.

The new year, 1773, started in a more pleasant way with two family marriages. In February, Avison's only surviving daughter, Jane, married at the age of 29. Her bridegroom was Avison's old friend, Robert Page, Deputy Controller of Customs. Page was a wealthy man, a Unitarian, an early opponent of slavery and instrumental in the foundation of the Literary and Philosophical Society in Newcastle, as well as a great lover of music. A month later, in March, Edward also married, to Margaret Dale (often known as

Peggy); Edward and Charles junior were supporters of Methodism, and Margaret was, for a short period, one of John Wesley's most frequent correspondents.[128]

But the celebrations were quickly followed by mourning; only four months later, in July, Jane died – the terms of her death notice in local papers suggests that, like her mother, she died of tuberculosis. It is unlikely that her illness was unknown at the time of her marriage; her husband, Robert Page, must surely have been aware that he was marrying a dying woman. Perhaps Page was continuing to look after the family of his old friend although he was certainly also aware that Jane was wealthy. He lived on until 1807; he never remarried but continued to help the younger generation of Avisons.

Both Edward and Charles junior may have had money worries in early 1774. Charles junior had held a benefit concert in April for the past three years but in 1774 he held two in quick succession, suggesting that the first had not been particularly profitable. In June, Edward advertised the sale, at reduced prices, of old editions of his father's music; this may have been simply to clear some space in the house, but may also have been to raise some money.

The winter subscription series went ahead in late 1774 but it seems to have been the last. Whether this was because of continuing disgruntlement with the terms of the subscription, or general lack of support is not clear; the influence and personal attractions of Avison may have kept the series afloat in earlier years – once this influence was removed many subscribers may have lost interest. In addition, Edward's health was probably poor; in 1775, he held only one concert in mid-year and then did not promote another until February 1776.

By this time, Charles junior's restlessness had become pronounced. In April 1776, he applied to his employers, the Corporation, for leave of absence to go abroad for a year, appointing a deputy to play at All Saints while he was away. All musicians with ambition took a trip to London early in their careers, for 'improvement', but Charles was planning to go further afield – to Russia.

Charles junior was almost certainly influenced by the travels of his cousin. Avison's niece, Ann (daughter of William in Hull), had married Richard Terry, a bright young man working for one of Hull's main shipping companies, and a successful Baltic merchant. Ann and Richard had six children, one of whom – Avison Terry – was twice Mayor of Hull.[129] William's son, also called William, had been apprenticed to a Russia merchant and in 1769 had set up on his own account, probably funded by his uncle Edward.[130] William had inherited the family love of music and subscribed to the music of Avison and Garth even while living abroad in Narva and Danzig. He seems to have invited Charles junior to travel with him; they went together to Russia and Charles probably lodged with William in Narva.[131] He was certainly there when his brother Edward died in October 1776, again most probably from tuberculosis.

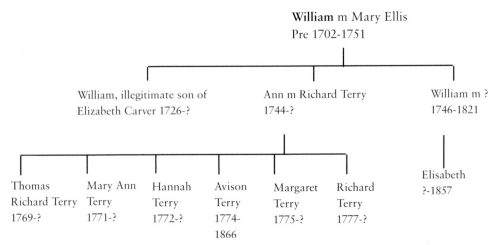

William m Mary Ellis
Pre 1702-1751

William, illegitimate son of Elizabeth Carver 1726-? | Ann m Richard Terry 1744-? | William m ? 1746-1821

Thomas Richard Terry 1769-? | Mary Ann Terry 1771-? | Hannah Terry 1772-? | Avison Terry 1774-1866 | Margaret Terry 1775-? | Richard Terry 1777-?

Elisabeth ?-1857

Edward's death broke the 40-year direct association of the Avison family with St Nicholas' church. Charles junior did not hurry back to claim the position of organist; he twice made excuses to stay in Russia, and, in September 1777, the Corporation became exasperated and dismissed him. However, the Avison connection did not disappear entirely, for the newly appointed organist at St Nicholas, Matthias Hawdon, was an old pupil of Charles's.

Charles junior does not seem to have returned to Newcastle until the end of 1779, by which time his sister-in-law, Edward's widow Margaret, was also dead, probably again of TB. Charles' wanderings in Russia may have cured him of his restlessness for he was now clearly intending to stay in the North East. He applied for, and was appointed to, the post of organist at All Saints, on the death of his father's old opponent, Solomon Strolger.

An anonymous writer to the *Newcastle Courant* (under the pseudonym of Clerimont) gives an interesting snapshot of Charles junior at this time.[132] The writer started by praising Charles' personal qualities, describing what he perceived as modern culture in surprisingly familiar terms: 'In this apostate age, when our youth is totally immersed in sensuality, 'tis a duty incumbent upon every well-wisher of the community, to promote the least appearance of industry in any individual who has had the courage to deviate from the licentious customs of the times.' Charles, he said, was 'deserving the greatest encouragement'. His simple style of playing (clearly following his father's principles) might at first seem 'a little singular' but he hoped it would make worshippers feel more devout than Strolger's 'unmeaning rants'. Rather patronisingly, he ended by suggesting that if the parishioners showed favour to and support for 'those branches of Society whose dependence rest solely upon their favour' – that is, the working classes – this might encourage them to emulate their betters and amend their behaviour.

The writer recommended the opening of a book of subscription for parishioners to contribute towards an increase in Charles' salary; the book was certainly opened but whether it made any real difference to Charles' financial situation is not known. By 1773, however, he felt sufficiently well-off to marry Catherine Wilson, from Newburn.

By this time, the character of musical life in Newcastle had changed considerably from the days of Charles Avison senior. Matthias Hawdon, who had taken over the post of organist at St Nicholas' Church, had promoted the mid-year and winter concerts from 1777; he seems to have been a bad financial manager and went bankrupt in 1781.[133] Although he came to an accommodation with his creditors and managed to carry on, his activities were greatly curtailed. He held very substantial and spectacular concerts in Assize Week when the town was full of visitors, almost guaranteeing a large audience and a good income, but cut the winter subscription series to only three concerts. In addition, he began to suffer ill-health.

Hawdon looked for assistance in concert promotion, and found it at Durham Cathedral. Thomas Ebdon, the cathedral organist, helped Hawdon to run a number of concerts then, in 1785, took over entirely when Hawdon became too ill to continue. Ebdon brought with him one of the cathedral singing men, Welshman Edward Meredith, who was rapidly becoming the darling of North Eastern audiences. [134]

Charles junior had little or no part in this activity, although he may have played in concerts; he certainly played in the theatre band, performing a solo on one occasion under the fashionably Italian alias of Carlos Avisonsini. He became very friendly with Edward Meredith and, in October 1783, held a joint benefit concert with him. This benefit was sponsored by the local freemasons

The new Assembly Rooms in Westgate Road opened in 1776 and was a popular venue for entertainments. The image is from Thomas Bewick's workshops.

and held in their hall in Newcastle; most musicians in the region were freemasons. The Freemasons also gave Charles a benefit on his own in 1785.

1783 was also notable for the death of Charles junior's uncle, the elder Edward – the last survivor of Richard and Ann's children. Edward senior was a wealthy man: his will, made in January 1778, mentioned property in the Castle Garth and on Northumberland Street as well as a great deal of money. This property was left to his widow for her lifetime but substantial bequests were made to all the nieces and nephews – to Charles junior, and Ann and William in Hull, and to their mother, Mary, and to various godchildren. Robert Page was made a trustee of the money to be paid to Charles junior, who received an annuity of £27 a year.[135]

The year after Edward senior's death, Charles named his eldest son for him; a second son, Charles, was born two years later and a daughter, Ann, in 1788. This increasing family may have exacerbated Charles's financial difficulties, for his income remained small. He received £20 a year as organist of All Saints, and was usually the beneficiary of an annual collection in appreciation of his work in teaching the parish children to sing psalms and hymns. He no doubt also had a teaching practice which brought in extra income and the Freemasons concerts would also have helped. Unlike his father, however, Charles junior was no composer and therefore derived no extra income from publication; he may well have composed solos for his own performance but the only surviving book published in his name was a book of psalms sung by the children of All Saints parish. The book was words only, published without tunes.[136]

Nor could Charles derive much income from performance. In 1785 Matthias Hawdon gave up concert promotion entirely, claiming that there was no longer any public support for concerts; Thomas Ebdon and Edward Meredith of Durham tried for a year or two more to prove him wrong but eventually gave up. After 1787, there was no winter subscription series and the only concerts were occasional benefits for Meredith. Musicians in the area could still look to engagements in the bands at the theatre and at the dancing assemblies, but there was not work for everyone.

Charles was incurring a number of debts which he could not pay, despite repeated reminders from his creditors. One of those owed money was the engraver, Thomas Bewick. Bewick's work on his natural history books, illustrated by his own painstaking miniatures and engravings, was supplemented by more mundane jobs, one of which was the printing of concert tickets for almost all the musicians in the region. Charles junior had ordered a large number of tickets from Bewick for the Freemasons' concert in 1783, asking for a plate to be engraved at a cost of 15 shillings, and 200 tickets to be printed from it for a further three shillings. Two packs of business cards cost him two shillings more and the bill came to a total of one guinea.

Charles did not pay. Nor did he pay a similar debt incurred in 1787 when, for another concert, he ordered 100 tickets (50 in black and 50 in a more expensive red) and two packs of cards. By this time he owed Bewick £1 10s 10d, and the engraver lost patience, taking out a summons against Charles and adding 6d to the bill for the legal costs. Charles paid off nine shillings of the debt, probably from the proceeds of the concert, but he still owed the balance of the debt in 1793. Bewick did not print any more tickets for him.[137]

In 1789, Charles' position improved when Matthias Hawdon died. Hawdon's son, Thomas, who had been working in Dundee and Hull, came home to take over Hawdon's teaching practice but in the selection of a new organist for St Nicholas' church, Charles was the one who triumphed. In September 1789, Charles stepped into the position once occupied by his father and by his dead brother, at a salary of £50 a year. His old position as organist at All Saints was taken over by Thomas Hawdon; the two men clearly became good friends despite the 14 years' difference between them – Charles was 38 years old, Thomas Hawdon 24.

The position of promoter of concerts in Newcastle had become inextricably associated with that of organist of St Nicholas; in 1790, Charles plunged into the task of organising a winter subscription series, enlisting Thomas Hawdon's help as co-promoter. If Charles anticipated the success that had been his father's, he was very disappointed. In 1785, Matthias Hawdon had said bitterly that there was not enough local interest to support a subscription series, and the situation had probably not changed. Charles and Thomas only attempted a three-concert series but their success was apparently not great.

They may well have continued to run the series in 1791 and 1792 but when Thomas died in 1793, at the age of only 28, Charles seems to have lost heart; in 1794, the subscription series was promoted by another local musician. The political situation only made matters worse. After the Revolution in France in 1789, relations between England and France continued to deteriorate until war broke out in 1793; inflation soared; almost every family had a member actively involved in the war. There was a general feeling that public entertainments were not appropriate in such serious times.

Charles had never achieved the eminence of his father and plainly was never going to achieve it. At the beginning of the 1790s, other local musicians were attaining prominence, and showing a flair for concert promotion, performance and composition that cast Charles junior into the shade. The new organist of All Saints, Thomas Thompson, was only 16 years old in 1794 but had studied in London with the pianist and composer, Muzeo Clementi; Thomas Wright, organist of St Andrew's and in his early 30s, was an admired clarinettist and a firm favourite with local audiences.

In midsummer 1794, Charles' financial position worsened when his salary as organist of St Nicholas' was cut from £50 to £30 per year.[138] Under the pressure of inflation and concern about the state of war with France, Charles'

employers, the
Corporation, were
cutting back their
expenses as much as they
could – the post of wait
was also abolished at this
time.

By this time, Charles
and Catherine had had
six children. Their eldest
son, Edward, died in
1794, aged ten; he seems
to have inherited the family's musical talents, being described in local papers as
'a boy of promising genius'. Their second son, Charles, lived only three years,
while another boy, called Robert Page after Charles' widowed brother-in-law,
did not live to his first birthday. At the beginning of 1795, the couple had three
surviving children, Ann Jane, aged seven, Jane (of unknown age) and a second
Charles, aged four. To sustain a family of five in such difficult times, when
demand for music was diminishing, must have been daunting. In one respect,
however, there was good news. Public music-making might have been regarded
as too trivial for such serious times but domestic music-making – a little dance
music after dinner, or a song or two in the family circle – was considered
unexceptional and many wealthy tradespeople were buying instruments and
looking for tuition. For a competent music teacher this was a good time.

In the event, it did not matter. On April 9, 1795, Charles junior died, at the
age of 53. The cause of death is not recorded.

~

After his death, all Charles junior's furniture and musical instruments,
including the harpsichord inherited from his father, were put up for sale at his
house in Lisle Street, to pay off his apparently numerous creditors. Robert Page
may well have bought a number of the more personal items to save them for
the family. The estate was still not settled two years later when creditors
claimed that Charles' widow, Catherine, was keeping back some of the money
that should strictly have gone to pay off Charles's debts. If this was indeed the
case, it is hard to blame Catherine; not only had she three children surviving at
Charles' death but she was pregnant with another, Catherine Abigail. In

addition, she suffered the death of one of her children, Jane, the year after Charles died.

Three of Charles' and Catherine's children survived to adulthood. Ann Jane married a currier, James Bell, after whose family two courts, one off Pilgrim Street and one off Newgate Street, were named. James and Ann lived in Bell Court off Newgate Street, with their two sons; in 1807, Catherine was also living there when she received an inheritance – the annual income on £1000 – left to her by Robert Page, who never forgot or neglected the family of his old friend.

Catherine's and Charles' only surviving son, the second son called Charles, named for his father and grandfather, may have been a keen musical amateur but, like his brother-in-law, he earned his living as a currier; the two men may have been in partnership as Charles lived in Bell's Court off Pilgrim Street. His household included his wife, Elizabeth, and his sister, Charles junior's posthumous daughter, Catherine Abigail. Catherine earned a living from making straw hats and selling them from a shop in Bell's Court, not very successfully.

In 1816, at the age of 25, Charles died; within a week of his death, his sister's shop was put up for sale – he had apparently been supporting her. Charles' collection of books, his music, a portrait (probably that of his grandfather) and two violins were sold to raise money for his widow.[139] He had no children, and with his death the main line of the family came to an end. The Avison family has no direct descendents in the male line.

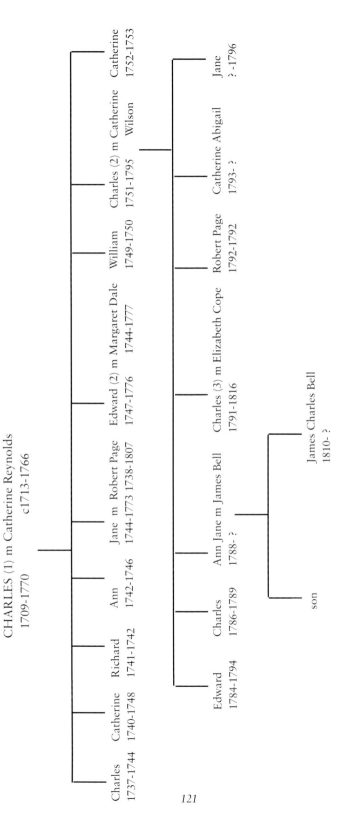

CHARLES (1) m Catherine Reynolds
1709-1770   c1713-1766

Charles
1737-1744

Catherine
1740-1748

Richard
1741-1742

Ann
1742-1746

Jane m Robert Page
1744-1773 1738-1807

Edward (2) m Margaret Dale
1747-1776   1744-1777

William
1749-1750

Charles (2) m Catherine
1751-1795   Wilson

Catherine
1752-1753

Jane
?-1796

Edward
1784-1794

Charles
1786-1789

Ann Jane m James Bell
1788- ?

Charles (3) m Elizabeth Cope
1791-1816

Robert Page
1792-1792

Catherine Abigail
1793- ?

son

James Charles Bell
1810- ?

Legacy

'A claim to be remembered'
Newcastle Daily Journal, May 28, 1890

Eighteenth-century composers did not generally expect their work to survive for long after their death. Composition was so closely linked with performance that it was unlikely that it should. Solo performers frequently composed their own solos and concertos; once they were no longer around to perform these works, the music tended to be forgotten. The case of Handel, whose music not only survived but gained a new importance and significance, was unusual, and was promoted by the aura of nationalism and patriotism that the oratorios in particular accumulated over the years. In addition, fashions changed quickly and it was not until the end of the century that it was considered important to preserve music in older styles.

Charles Avison was luckier than most composers. At the end of the century, the aristocracy, faced with threats to their authority posed by the American and French Revolutions, attempted to bolster their position by posing as the arbiters of good taste and the protectors of traditional values. In music this meant support for so-called 'ancient' music. For some people this involved reviving the works of composers such as Palestrina and Byrd; for others it meant merely reasserting the virtues of Corelli and Geminiani and composers of their generation.[140]

This benefited Avison as a pupil of Geminiani; his music was regularly played by the Society of Ancient Music in London until around 1813. The undemanding nature of the orchestral writing, specifically aimed for Avison' mixed ensemble in Newcastle, also made it a continuing favourite of provincial players throughout the 19th century.

Critical opinion, however, was mixed. In the 19th century, critics heard Avison's music as light and elegant but wanting in originality. They suggested that he admired his old teacher, Geminiani, too much and followed him too slavishly; the implication was that the music was pleasant but lightweight. This opinion was strengthened by some 19th-century arrangements, particularly one of a melody from the third concerto from Opus 9, which was turned into a vocal piece called *Sound the loud Timbrel*. This became immensely popular but reviewers damned it; one referred to it as 'a delicious morsel for the young ladies'.[141]

In the late 19th century, however, Avison's cause was championed by the poet Robert Browning who remembered with delight playing as a child an Avison march (possibly the march written for the Yorkshire Buffs). Browning's testimonial encouraged a renewal of interest in Newcastle and a proposal was made to restore the stone on the Avisons' grave in St Andrew's churchyard.

The original tombstone recorded the deaths of Avison and Catherine and that of their daughter Jane in Latin; the wording suggests that it was erected by Jane's widower, Robert Page, and perhaps replaced an earlier stone that recorded only Avison's and Catherine's deaths. A reference to Charles junior was added, in English, after his death in 1795 and Page himself was added 14 years later – the inscription reverted to Latin for Page. Finally, in 1816, the details of the life of the youngest Charles, grandson of the composer, were inscribed.

In 1890, all these inscriptions were copied onto a new stone, together with a verse from Browning's tribute, describing Avison as

... on the list
Of worthies who by help of pipe or wire
Expressed in sound rough rage or soft desire.[142]

A note recording the date of restoration completed the inscription and the new stone was placed on top of the original.

The dedication of the restored stone, on May 28, 1890, was accompanied by extensive ceremony. William Ions, the organist of St Nicholas' church (now a cathedral) gave an organ recital which included concertos 1, 2 and 8 from Opus 9 and a voluntary in D minor from what was described as 'Avison's pocket manuscript book' which is probably one of the notebooks now preserved in Newcastle's City Library.

The new stone was then unveiled by Judge Digby Seymour who was president of the restoration movement. Seymour was full of other ideas for preserving Avison's name, suggesting a tablet in St Nicholas, or the funding of a professorship or studentship in his name at Armstrong College. Sadly,

Browning was not present as he had died five months previously, but he had known of the movement to restore the stone and approved of it; his son, R. Barrett Browning, had sent a letter remarking that 'my father was really pleased to think he had been able to call attention to Charles Avison with such good result'.[143]

Outside Avison's home town, however, critical judgement remained ambivalent or openly adverse. In the early 1970s, Arthur Hutchings, in his book *The Baroque Concerto*, damned with faint praise. After describing Avison himself as 'charming, inspiring, and altogether admirable', he described his music as 'even less imaginative' than Geminiani's (thus managing to condemn both composers at once) and pedantic. He did, however, admire one or two isolated movements of the concertos.[144]

For the most part, the late 19th and early 20th centuries neglected Avison's music although occasional performances did take place in Newcastle, particularly in the late 1960s when the Northern Sinfonia orchestra played the concertos several times. They celebrated the 200th anniversary of Avison's death in 1970 with a concert at St Nicholas' church and a tribute on the BBC Third programme.

The revival of Charles Avison's music did not take off, however, until 1984. At that time cellist Gordon Dixon and viola player Colin Start discovered some parts to an Avison concerto and realised that his music was largely unknown. Supported by Start, Dixon founded the Avison Ensemble with the intention of finding out more about Avison's music through playing it and promoting it to a wider audience.

A concert at St John's church, in aid of the Ethiopian Famine Appeal, was followed over the next few years by concerts in Newcastle and at Hexham, Brighton and elsewhere. Interest gathered and in 1991 the Charles Avison Society was launched to support the Ensemble and to encourage interest in Avison and his music. In 1994, the Lord Mayor of Newcastle unveiled the Society's plaque on the wall of St Andrew's churchyard, and the Avison Ensemble inaugurated their first regular series of concerts, now using period instruments to attempt to reproduce the original sound and performing style of the music as closely as possible.

Towards the close of 2000, the Ensemble and Society were astonished to hear of the survival of a unique document. All composers use notebooks in which to jot down their ideas, to sketch out works, or to note down the music of other composers. Such a notebook, alleged to belong to Avison, had just come to light and was being offered for sale at Sotheby's. Hurried negotiations not only confirmed that the notebook had indeed almost certainly been Avison's, but also raised enough money to purchase it.

Pledges of £11,500 were raised from members of the Society itself in under a fortnight and the Heritage Lottery Fund promised the balance up to a hammer price of £50,000. Unfortunately, the book was sold to a foreign buyer and there was a danger that it would leave the country. Working with the British Library, a plan was drafted to stop an export licence being granted, but before that was put in place, the American buyer decided to sell the book to the Avison Ensemble for the total auction price of £52,250.

Even more astonishingly, a second notebook came to light in 2002. This too, was purchased by the Society, again with the assistance of members of the Avison Society and Heritage Lottery Fund support; both books were conserved by experts at Northumbria University and form a central part of the new Avison Archive set up in conjunction with Newcastle Libraries. The workbooks contain a number of unpublished arrangements by Avison, and the Avison Ensemble have now committed these to CD. The City of Newcastle celebrates Charles Avison in naming the 2009 new City Library 'The Charles Avison Building'.

~

Charles Avison's music is still being played in Newcastle (and increasingly elsewhere) and is again reaching a wider audience. For the first time recordings of all of his published compositions are available from the Avison Ensemble. These, carefully researched and presented in as authentic a style as possible, now allow modern music-lovers to hear the music as Avison and his audiences could have heard it, and to appreciate its attractions and virtues. As Avison himself said, in his *Essay on Musical Expression*:

> *[Their] Elegance of Taste ... consists not in those agile Motions, or Shiftings of the Hand which strike with Surprize the common Ear, but in the tender and delicate Touches, which ... to a fine Ear [are] productive of the Highest Delight.*[145]

Notes

1 Roz Southey, *Music-Making in North-East England During the Eighteenth Century* (London: Ashgate, 2006).

2 Westgate Street is now Westgate Road.

3 All details of the Avison family history come from parish registers. For details of Newcastle at the period, the best source is Henry Bourne, *The History of Newcastle upon Tyne or the Ancient and Present State of that Town* (Newcastle upon Tyne: John White, 1736). Bourne was chaplain of All Saints (All Hallows) until his death in 1733; his book, published posthumously in 1735, paints a vivid picture of the town at this period.

4 Details about waits come from the records of their employers, the Corporation. The Chamberlain's accounts of the Corporation of Newcastle upon Tyne (Tyne and Wear Archive Service [TWAS] 543/74-154 record details of their salaries and other payments; the Common Council minutes of Newcastle Corporation [TWAS] give details of appointments, dismissals and deaths, and other events.)

5 Joseph Taylor, *A Journey to Edenborough in Scotland* (Edinburgh: William Brown, 1903), 87-90.

6 York record Office: Chamberlain's Accounts, York Corporation, Vol. 35, October 18, 1736.

7 TWAS Common Council Minutes Newcastle Corporation, October 8, 1705.

8 TWAS Common Council Minutes April 17, 1711.

9 His widow collected and signed a receipt for his last half year's pay on December 26, 1721. TWAS, DF.OX/9/1.

10 The organists of All Saints and St Nicholas' were paid by the Newcastle Corporation and details of their appointments and payments to them can be found in the Chamberlain's Accounts and in Common Council minutes.

11 For details of François Prendecourt's career, see Edward T. Corps, 'Further Light on the Career of "Captain" François de Prendcourt', *Music and Letters*, lxxviii (1997), 15-23.

12 Information on James Hesletine's career at Durham Cathedral can be found in Cathedral Archives now kept by Durham University Library. These records include the Treasurer's Accounts of Durham Cathedral and the Act Books of the Dean and Chapter of Durham Cathedral.

13 The National Archive, (TNA) IRI 44/118.

14 East Riding of Yorkshire Archives and Records Service, PE 158/421.

15 Ann's signature on the receipt for the salary is sometimes used as evidence that Ann herself was organist at Gateshead, but this is unlikely. It was not unusual for family members to collect salaries for musicians in case of illness or death.

16 Six Sonatas for two violins and a bass (London: Benjamin Cooke, c1737). For the suggestion that Avison was apprenticed to Jenison see Norris Lynn Stephens, *Charles Avison, An Eighteenth-Century English Composer, Musician and Writer* (University of Pittsburgh, PhD dissertation, 1968), 1-4.

17 Records from Admission Books for 1710-1733 survive as do Guild Books for 1709-21 and

from 1755 onwards. Edward Avison's later admission in 1728 is recorded there. If Charles Avison was apprenticed in Newcastle it should be around age 14 and he should be admitted around the age of 21, both of which should be covered by these surviving records. *Register of Freemen of Newcastle upon Tyne*, ed. Arthur Maule Oliver, Publications of the Newcastle upon Tyne Records Committee, 6 (Newcastle: Northumberland Press, 1926).

18 Musical life in eighteenth-century London has been widely researched although more at the end of the century than at the beginning. Simon McVeigh offers a brief account of the early part of the century in *Concert Life in London from Mozart to Haydn* (Cambridge: Cambridge University Press, 1993); Jenny Burchell's *Polite or Commercial Concerts? Concert management and Orchestral Repertoire in Edinburgh, Bath, Oxford, Manchester, and Newcastle, 1730-1799* (New York and London: Garland Publishing, 1996) also gives a full account of concert life in provincial towns and in Edinburgh.

19 *York Courant* 19 August 19, 1760.

20 Details of Elford's career at Durham Cathedral can be found in Treasurer's Accounts and Dean and Chapter Minutes, Durham Cathedral Archive.

21 If Edward's violin was indeed meant for Avison at Jenison's house in October 1733, it argues that Avison's departure for London was after that date. A stay of about a year in London would have been a normal occurrence.

22 Charles Burney, *A General History of Music* (London: 1776). Burney obtained his information from Ann Ord (see Chapter 9) and it is not known if he double-checked the accuracy of his informant; as he was working against time to get his *History* published before that of his competitor, Sir John Hawkins, it is unlikely that he did so. Burney was also inconsistent in his attitude to Avison, having written favourably of him in 1753; by the time he wrote the history in the 1770s, however, he wrote that Avison's compositions 'want force, correctness and originality' and accused him of over-rating Marcello either in order to depreciate Handel or to increase the market for Garth's arrangements of the psalms. Burney, *A General History*, vol. 4, 582, 670: Charles Burney, *The Letters of Dr Charles Burney*, Vol. 1: 1751-1784, ed. Alvaro Ribiero (Oxford: Clarendon Press, 1991), 12.

23 Letters in Scotland and Charles Avison, *An Essay on Musical Expression* (London: C. Davis, 1752), 76.

24 Enrico Careri, 'Geminiani, Francesco', Grove Music Online, http://www.grovemusic.com (Accessed February 11, 2008).

25 *Newcastle Courant*, September 17, 1768.

26 Arthur H. Scouten (ed.), *The London Stage 1660-1800* (Carbondale, Illinois: S. Illinois University Press, 1961), Part 3, 1729-1747, 278: *Delia and Thyrsis* survives in one of Avison's notebooks, now in Newcastle City Library. (See Chapter 17)

27 Details of Mountier's career at Durham can be found in the Treasurer's Accounts and Dean and Chapter Minutes of Durham Cathedral

28 TWAS, Gu.Ty/13/3.

29 Information about concerts in the North East region comes largely from local newspapers: the *Newcastle Courant*, *Newcastle Journal*, *Newcastle Advertiser* and other shorter-lived papers. The first of these, the *Courant*, appeared in 1712; details about concerts and other musical

events before this time must be gleaned therefore from private papers and are few and far between.

30 *Newcastle Courant* May 19-21, 1712.

31 *Newcastle Courant* May 22, 1725. The Grammar School had once been the Chapel of St Mary's Hospital. A statue of George Stephenson now stands on the site.

32 *Newcastle Courant* September 29, November 10, December 1, 1733.

33 George Bowes and his second wife, Mary, kept accounts recording all their expenditure; these survive in Durham County Record Office and give details of their musical activities, in London and in the North-East. Strathmore Papers, Durham County Record Office, (DRO) D/St/E15/5/67-100. See also Roz Southey, *The Bowes of Gibside – the Musical Activities of a North-Eastern Gentry Family, 1730-1760* [forthcoming]

34 *Newcastle Courant* September 20, 1735.

35 *Newcastle Courant* 10, 17, 24 April, 8, 15, 22, 29 May 1736.

36 *Newcastle Courant* May 22, 1736.

37 *Newcastle Courant* May 22, 1736.

38 *Newcastle Courant* May 29, 1736.

39 Common Council Minutes, Newcastle Corporation, March 23, 1737.

40 The discussion of church music and the organist's duties can be found in footnotes in Charles Avison, *An Essay on Musical Expression*, (London: C. Davis, 1752), 75-78.

41 *Newcastle Courant* January 13, 1780. Information about Strolger can be found in Treasurer's Accounts of Newcastle Corporation; also in Rosemary Southey, *Commercial music-making in 18th century North-East England: A Pale Reflection of London?* PhD Dissertation, University of Newcastle upon Tyne, 2001.

42 *Newcastle Journal* May 5, 1739.

43 Information on the homes occupied by the Avisons at various times usually comes from newspaper advertisements; it was common practice to end these advertisements with details of where tickets for concerts could be obtained and this usually included Avison's home address.

44 *Newcastle Courant* January 21, 1738.

45 *Newcastle Journal* November 4-11, 1758.

46 Southey, *Commercial music-making*, 55-59.

47 *Newcastle Courant* July 29, 1738.

48 *Newcastle Journal* November 4-11, 1758

49 Avison, *Essay*, 112-138.

50 Ibid., 125-6.

51 Ibid., 137.

52 The 18th century Bigg Market was larger than the present street, taking a dog's leg at one end; the Turk's Head stood where Nun Street now meets Grainger Street.

53 *Newcastle Journal* November 4-11, 1758.

54 *Literary Register* (1769), 207.

55 *Newcastle Journal* March 17, 1759.

56 Six Sonatas for two violins and a bass, Opus 1 (London: Benjamin Cooke, c1737).

57 Roz Southey, 'The Role of Gentlemen Amateurs in Subscription Concerts in North-East England during the Eighteenth Century', in *Music in the British Provinces, 1690-1914* ed. Rachel Cowgill and Peter Holman (London: Ashgate, 2007) 115-128.

58 Blathwayt, formerly Director of the Royal Academy of Music in London, and his elder brother, William of Dyrham Park in Gloucestershire, had visited Newcastle as young men in 1703 when they heard the waits playing, probably including Richard Avison.

59 William Gilpin, *Memoirs of Dr Richard Gilpin, of Scaleby Castle in Cumberland; And of his Posterity in the Two Succeeding Generations; Written in the Year 1791, by the Rev Wm. Gilpin, Vicar of Boldre: Together with an Account of the Author, by Himself: And a Pedigree of the Gilpin Family,* ed. William Jackson (London: Bernard Quaritch, 1879); Madam d'Arblay [Fanny Burney], *Memoirs of Doctor Burney,* 3 vols. (London: Edward Moxon, 1832), III, 101.

60 William Roberts, *A Dawn of Imaginative Feeling* (Carlisle: Northern Academic Press, 1996), 86-119; East Riding of Yorkshire Archives and Records Service, DDGR/42/16/69); *Biographia Britannica,* 7 vols (London: W. Innys, 1747-66), II (1749), 653-676.

61 Jane Ellison left Jane Avison an annuity of £10 in her will but the estate could not meet her many bequests, and Avison, on Jane's behalf, agreed to a one-off payment instead. DRO D/Br/D939 (Jane Ellison's will); D/Br/D948, June 11, 1761 (bond between Charles Avison and Henry Ellison of Gateshead Park).

62 Stanley Sadie, 'Garth, John,' Grove Music Online, http://www.grovemusic.com (Accessed June 20, 2008).

63 See Chapter 5.

64 It is difficult to assess the length of Avison's visits to Gibside from the accounts; the fact that he was paid only once a year does not mean he was paid for only one visit – the sum may have been for weekly lessons, for instance. The only sure evidence for the length of visits is when he was given payments over several days.

65 Gibside is still the scene of large-scale musical events; the Northern Sinfonia holds an annual outdoor concert there in July.

66 Six Concertos in Seven Parts for Four Violins, one Alto Viola, a Violoncello and a thorough Bass for the Harpsichord, Opus 3 (London: John Johnson, 1751).

67 William Hayes of Oxford called the presentation of Opus 3 with its preface as being 'ushered into the world in so pompous a Manner'. For information on William Hayes's reaction to Avison's ideas, see Pierre Dubois (ed.), *Charles Avison's Essay on Musical Expression: With Related Writings by William Haye and Charles Avison* (London: Ashgate, 2004).

68 *Newcastle Courant* November 10-17, Newcastle Journal November 17, 1750.

69 Common Council Minutes, Newcastle Corporation, June 26, 1749.

70 Northumberland Record Office (NRO) 324/E/7, 10, 11, 15, 16, 20.

71 Charles Avison, *An Essay in Musical Expression* (London: C. Davis, 1752).

72 For a full account of Hayes's objections and writings, see Pierre Dubois (ed.), *Charles Avison's Essay on Musical Expression, with related Writings by William Hayes and Charles Avison* (London: Ashgate, 2004).

73 *Mr Avison's Reply to the Author of Remarks on His Essay on Musical Expression, &c.,* Charles Avison, *An Essay in Musical Expression*, 2nd Edition (London: C. Davis, 1753).

74 Spencer Cowper, *Letters of Spencer Cowper, Dean of Durham, 1746-1774*, ed. Edward Hughes, Surtees Society Publications 165 (Durham/London: Andrew and Co.,/Barnard Quaritch, 1950); Roz Southey, 'Competition and Collaboration: Concert Promotion in Newcastle and Durham, 1752-1772' in *Concert Life in Eighteenth-Century Britain* ed. Susan Wollenberg and Simon McVeigh (London: Ashgate, 2004) 55-70.

75 Story recounted by Spencer Cowper, in Letters, 168. For details of Giardini's career, see Simon McVeigh, 'Felice Giardini: A violinist in late eighteenth-century London', *Music and Letters*, Vol. lxiv, 162-172.

76 Charles Burney, *A General History of Music* (London: T. Beckett, 1776-1789), IV (1789), 640. See also Owain Edwards, 'Espionage, a Collection of Violins, and Le Bizarre Universalie: a Fresh Look at William Corbett.' *Musical Quarterly*, vol. 73 (1989), 320-43.

77 TWAS: HO/RVI/22.

78 See note 62.

79 Thomas Gray, *Correspondence of Thomas Gray*, Ed. Paget Toynbee and Leonard Whibley, 3 vols. (Oxford: Clarendon Press, 1938), I, 418-9.

80 Eight Concertos in Seven Parts, Opus 4 (London: John Johnson, 1955).

81 *A Collection of Psalm Tunes in Two Parts, Adapted to the several Meters in the Old and New Version, and to those in Dr Watts's Translation, Revised and Corrected by Mr Avison* (Newcastle upon Tyne, William Charnley, 1757): [in copy of 18th edition of Isaac Watts, *The Psalms of David*].

82 Avison had announced this project at the end of the second edition of *An Essay on Musical Expression* in 1753.

83 Letter to Dr Bever in Oxford, in the possession of the Royal College of Music, Mss 2, 169; quoted in Stephens, *Charles Avison*, 179.

84 In 1791, the organiser of concerts in York was forced to change to wax candles for the same reason, a serious matter in view of the facts that the series was in severe financial trouble at the time. *York Chronicle* January 28, 1791.

85 Mr Charles the Hungarian clarinettist had taken part in subscription concerts in Durham and Newcastle in late 1754, and held benefits for himself in Durham, Newcastle and Hexham at the same period. (*Newcastle Courant* October 26, November 9, November 23, 1754.) The clarinet was a new instrument at this time, appealing to audiences' love of novelties. The Passerinis, Giuseppe and Christina, had briefly stayed in Newcastle in May 1752 (*Newcastle Courant* May 23, 1752).

86 *Newcastle Journal* November 4-11, 1758.

87 *Newcastle Journal* March 17, 1759.

88 Published 1766.

89 Avison and Garth had witnessed the addition of a codicil to George Bowes's will two years earlier. TNA, PROB 11/870.

90 We are grateful to Lesley Richard, Assistant Keeper of Fine and Decorative Art, Laing Art

Gallery, Newcastle, and Joanna Hashagan, Keeper of Textiles, Bowes Museum, Barnard Castle, Co. Durham for their advice on the portrait.

91 Christopher Wright, compiler, *British and Irish Paintings in Public Collections* (New Haven: Yale University Press, 2006), 526. A notice of the death of Francis Lindo, Esq of Isleworth, appeared in *The Gentleman's Magazine*, 37 (1767), 144; it is not clear whether this was indeed the painter.

92 It has been suggested that the absence of a wig in a portrait often signified an independent-minded man; vagaries of fashion have to be taken into account however and Avison's clothes in the portrait are much as would have been expected at the time.

93 The Garden concerts in Newcastle are known only from newspaper advertisements; the appearance of the gardens themselves can only be gleaned from later maps which show the approximate shape and the locations of the buildings.

94 TWAS, 575/3/20a/51.

95 Avison, *Essay*, 70-71.

96 Grimston subscribed to Avison's Opus 9 in March 1766 [East Yorkshire Archives DDGR/42/16/23] and was a correspondent of John Brown [DDGR/42/16/19].

97 The story of William Herschel's early musical activities is told by his great grand-daughter, Constance Lubbock, in her book *The Herschel Chronicle: The Life-Story of William Herschel and his sister, Caroline Herschel* (Cambridge: Cambridge University Press, 1933), 14-22.

98 *Newcastle Courant* October 2, 1762.

99 *Newcastle Journal* April 16-23, April May 7, May 7-14 1763.

100 *Newcastle Courant*, September 3, 17, 1763.

101 Avison also produced a Dirge based on words written by David Garrick for an extra scene in a performance of *Romeo and Juliet*. A copy of this duet for two sopranos survives at Burghley House.

102 Simon McVeigh, 'Music and the Lock Hospital in the 18th century', *The Musical Times*, Vol. 129, No. 1743 (May 1988), 235-6 and 239-240.

103 D. Burrows and R. Dunhill, *Music and Theatre in Handel's World: the Family Papers of James Harris, 1732-1780* (Oxford: Oxford University Press, 2002), 438.

104 The details of the Green Court house can be deduced from bequests in Charles's will.

105 *The Will of a Certain Northern Vicar ...* (London: printed for the Author, 1765).

106 *The Will of a certain Northern Vicar. The Second Edition, with Corrections. To which is Annex'd, a Codicil, &c.* (London: for the Author, 1765).

107 This poem does not survive but its existence can be deduced from another pamphlet: *A Caveat to the Will of a Certain Northern Vicar. Addressed to the Reverend W. C*****, Rector of K**** W***** (London: W. Flexney, 1766). In this pamphlet, a man called 'Charles' is described extensively and includes the lines: 'Ingrateful man! Who bless'd with ev'ry pow'r/To lift the soul beyond the Muses' bow'r,/What would he more? If honour waits him here,/Why seek distinction in the poet's sphere?'

108 *Newcastle Courant* December 7, 1765.

109 'Letter from a Gentleman to his friend [Lord Lyttleton] in London', *The London Chronicle*,

April 24, 1766.

110 William Gilpin, *Observations Relative Chiefly to Picturesque Beauty, Made in the Year 1772, on Several Parts of England, particularly the Mountains and Lakes of Cumberland and Westmoreland* (London, 1786).

111 *Journal Britannique*, 5 (1751), 291-317.

112 Uta Janssons, *Matthieu Maty and the Journal Britannique, 1750-1755: a French View of English Literature in the middle of the Eighteenth Century* (Amsterdam: Holland University Press, 1975), 31. Maty's publication of a review of the *Essay* in the *Journal Britannique* may have encouraged interest in Charles's compositions in France and may explain performances of his work there. (See Chapter 4)

113 *Newcastle Courant* October 18, 1766.

114 *Twelve Concertos (divided into two sets) for Two Violins, one Alto Viola, and a Violoncello. This Work is also Adapted to the Practice of the Organ or Harpsichord alone Or these to serve as an Accompanyment to the Parts in Concerts which may be Reinforced at Pleasure*, Opus 9 (London: for the Author, 1766 and 1767).

115 The composer's full name was Giovanni Carlo Maria Clari; he is more commonly referred to as Giovanni nowadays.

116 Twelve Canticles taken from the Compositions of Carlo Clari and adapted to English and Selected from the Psalms. Collections 1 and 2, Newcastle 1769. Avison cited Addison's comments on English Psalms in the *Spectator* in support of the project.

117 *Literary Register*, I (1769), 278.

118 *Literary Register,* I (1769), 255.

119 Though these were written over initials, the internal evidence suggests that these contributions were by Avison; they also cease at the time of his death. They cover questions of interest to him: religion, literature, patronage, Geminiani, and a defence of his friend John Brown (perhaps the best evidence, as it mentions their acquaintance of almost thirty years, which is known to be correct from their meeting at Carlisle). His letters appear on the following pages of the *Literary Register*: under AC in I (1769), pp. 103, 119, 128, 145, 166, 168, 177, 187, 207, 212, 223, 247, 255, 262, 301: in II (1770), on 37, 71-2, 77, 93, 99, 104: under CA in I (1769) on 231, 278, 284, 295.

120 *Literary Register* I (1769) 168.

121 *Newcastle Courant* May 12, 1770.

122 TNA PROB 11/360

123 *Newcastle Journal* 25 May 25- September 1, 1770.

124 *Literary Register*, I (1769), 155.

125 *Newcastle Courant* April 6, 1771.

126 *Newcastle Courant* September 21, 1771.

127 Miss Alphi's mid year concerts were advertised in the *Newcastle Courant* and *Newcastle Chronicle* of August 15 and the *Newcastle Journal* of August 8-15 1772; her marriage in the *Courant* and *Chronicle* of October 3, and her withdrawal from the winter series, on account of 'being very unexpectedly prevented from attending' in the *Courant* and *Chronicle* of October 3

and the *Journal* of September 26-October 3, 1772.

128 *Newcastle Chronicle* February 20, 1773 (Jane's marriage); *Newcastle Courant* March 6, 1773 (Edward's marriage); *Newcastle Courant* July 17, 1773 (death of Jane).

129 Gordon Jackson, *Hull in the Eighteenth Century, A Study in Economic and Social History* (London: Oxford University Press, 1972), 49, 101-102, 144.

130 In 1769, Avison sent a note to the *Literary Register* recounting an instance of 'private generosity' in which a gentleman 'who has a family of his own, and not possessed of a considerable fortune, has sold a pleasant little villa and estate, to raise some money for the support of a deserving nephew, who had served his time to a Russia merchant'. *Literary Register* I (1769), 262.

131 St. Mariæ sogn, Helsingør, Døde mænd fra 1821 til dec. 1822 <http://home20.inet.tele.dk/winnie2/doedmolai1821.html.> [accessed May 19, 2007].

Elisabeth Avison of Helsingor (Elsinore, in Denmark) died unmarried c1857, leaving her entire estate to her Terry relatives; she was probably William's only child. William junior was to spend the rest of his life in the Russia trade, dying at Elsinore in 1821.

132 *Newcastle Courant* 13, January 20, 1780.

133 Thomas Bewick's ledgers and cash books provide information on tickets printed by Bewick for North Eastern musicians and survive in the Tyne and Wear Archives. The accommodation Matthias Hawdon reached with his creditors is recorded by Bewick in July 1881 (TWAS 1269/22).

134 Southey, *Commercial Music-Making*, 181-185.

135 TNA, PROB 11/1110.

136 Charles Avison, *A Collection of Hymns as sung by the Children of All Saints Church, Newcastle*, 2nd edition, (Newcastle: T. Angus, 1784).

137 Bewick's dealings with Charles junior are detailed in TWAS 1269/22.

138 TWAS 543/148 (1793-4).

139 *Newcastle Courant* September 14, 1816.

140 For the story of the rise of 'ancient' music and the idea of musical classics, see William Weber, *The Rise of Musical Classics in Eighteenth-Century England* (Oxford: Clarendon Press, 1992).

141 The comment appears in a review of a 1824 concert at the Concert of Ancient Music in The Harmonicon; quoted in P. M. Horsley, 'Charles Avison: The Man and his Milieu', *Music and Letters*, lv (1974), p. 12.

142 Browning's poem is rather less complimentary than this extract suggests, for the dots represent the omitted words 'not conspicuous'.

143 *Newcastle Daily Journal*, May 28, May 29, 1890.

144 Arthur Hutchings, *The Baroque Concerto* (London: Faber, 1973), 279-284.

145 Avison, *Essay*, 124.

Published compositions of Charles Avison

with details and dates of first publication

Six Sonatas for Two Violins and a Bass Opus 1 (London: Benjamin Cooke, c1737): dedicated to Ralph Jenison Esq.

Six Concertos in Seven Parts Opus 2 (Newcastle: Joseph Barber, 1740): dedicated to the Honourable Colonel Blathwayt.

Two Concertos, The First for an Organ or Harpsichord in Eight Parts, The Second for Violins in Seven Parts (Newcastle: Joseph Barber, 1742).

Twelve Concertos in Seven Parts for Four Violins, one Alto Viola, a Violoncello, and a Thorough Bass, done from two books of Lessons for the Harpsichord Composed by Sigr Domenico Scarlatti with additional slow Movements from Manuscript Solo Pieces by the Same Author (London: for the Author, 1744): dedicated to Mrs Bowes.

Eight Concertos for the Organ or Harpsichord (London: J. Walsh, 1747).

Six Concertos in Seven Parts for Four Violins, One Alto Viola, a Violoncello, and a Thorough Bass for the Harpsichord, with general Rules for Playing Instrumental Compositions in Parts, but more especially Calculated for the Use of this Work Opus 3 (London: John Johnson, 1751): dedicated to Mrs Ord.

Eight Concertos in Seven Parts Opus 4 (London: John Johnson, 1755): dedicated to Lady Milbanke.

Six Sonatas for the Harpsichord with Accompanyments for two Violins and Violoncello and a Thorough Bass for the Harpsichord Opus 5 (London: John Johnson, 1756): dedicated to Lady Blackett.

A Collection of Psalm Tunes in Two Parts, Adapted to the several Meters in the Old and New Version, and to those in Dr Watt's Translation, Revised and corrected by Mr Avison (Newcastle upon Tyne: William Charnley, 1757) (in copy of 18th edition of Isaac Watts, *The Psalms of David*).

Twelve Concertos in Seven Parts for Four Violins, one Alto-Viola, a Violoncello, and a Thorough Bass for the Harpsichord Opus 6 (Newcastle: for the Author, 1758). [Consisting of Opus 2 (revised) plus 2 new concertos published as *8 concertos for harpsichord or organ* (1747) all again revised plus 4 new concertos.]

Twenty Six Concertos Composed for Four Violins, one Alto Viola, a Violoncello, and Ripieno Bass, Divided into Four Books in Score, for the use of Performers On the Harpsichord (1758). [Consisting of Opuses 3, 4 and 6.]

Six Sonatas for the Harpsichord With Accompanyments, For Two Violins, and a Violoncello Opus 7 (Newcastle: for the Author, 1760).

Glory to God, Christmas Hymn (1767).

Six Sonatas for the Harpsichord with Accompanyments for two Violins and a Violoncello Opus 8 (London: for the Author, 1764): dedicated to Miss Bowes.

Twelve Concertos (Divided into two Sets) for Two Violins, One Alto Viola, and a Violoncello, This Work is also adapted to the Practice of the Organ or Harpsichord alone Or these to serve as an Accompanyment to the Parts in Concerts which may be Reinforced at Pleasure Opus 9 (London: for the Author, 1766).

Six Concertos in Seven Parts for Four Violins, one Alto Viola, a Violoncello, and a Thorough Bass for the Harpsichord Opus 10 (London: Robert Bremner, 1769).

Select discography

All recordings on CD unless otherwise stated.

Six Sonatas for Two Violins and a Bass (Opus 1); Six Sonatas for the Harpsichord with Accompanyments for two Violins and the Violoncello (Opus 8), The Avison Ensemble, directed by Pavlo Beznosiuk (Divine Art, 2009; dda 21214 [2 CDs]).

Concertos from Twenty-six Concertos (Nos 8, 9, 10, 12), Opus 2 (Nos 1, 3), Bournemouth Sinfonietta, directed by Ronald Thomas (HMV-EMI 1980; ASD 3842 [LP only]).

Six Concertos, Opus 3; Eight Concertos, Opus 4, The Avison Ensemble, directed by Pavlo Beznosiuk (Naxos, 2006; 8.557905-06 [2 CDs]).

Six Sonatas for the harpsichord with Accompanyments for two Violins and Violoncello (Opus 5); Six Sonatas for the Harpsichord with Accompanyments for Two Violins and a Violoncello (Opus 7), The Avison Ensemble, directed by Pavlo Beznosiuk (Divine Art, 2009; dda 21215 [2 CDs]).

Six Concertos from Opus 6 (Nos 1, 2, 6, 8, 9, 12) Hurwitz Chamber Ensemble, directed by Emanuel Hurwitz (L'Oiseau-Lyre (Decca), 1971; SOL 318 [LP only]).

Twelve Concertos Opus 6, The Avison Ensemble, directed by Pavlo Beznosiuk (Naxos, 2004; 8.557553-54 [2 CDs]).

12 Concerti for Strings after Domenico Scarlatti, L'Ensemble Berlin (Koch-Schwann, 1985, 2002; 3-131 8-2 [two CDs]).

4 Concerti Grossi after Domenico Scarlatti, Nos 2, 4, 6, 12, Tafel music Baroque Orchestra, directed by Jean Lamon (CBC Enterprises, 1987; SMCD 5061).

12 Concerti Grossi (1744) after sonatas by Domenico Scarlatti, The Brandenburg Consort, directed by Roy Goodman (Hyperion, 1994; CDA 66891/2 [two CDs]).

Concertos in Seven Parts from the Lessons of Domenico Scarlatti, No 3, 5, 6, 9, 11, 12, Café Zimmermann, directed by Pablo Valetti (Alpha, 2002; 031).

12 Concerti Grossi after Scarlatti, Academy of St Martin in the Fields directed by Sir Neville Marriner (Philips, 1993; 438806-2 [2 CDs]).

12 Concerti Grossi after Scarlatti, The Avison Ensemble, directed by Pavlo Beznosiuk (Divine Art, 2008; dda 21213 [2CDs]).

Concerti from Opus 9, Nos 1, 4, 6, 7, 8, 9, The Georgian Consort, leader Simon Jones (Divine Art, 2001; 2-4108).

12 Concerti Grossi (Opus 9); 6 Concerti Grossi (Opus 10), The Avison Ensemble, directed by Pavlo Beznosiuk (Divine Art, 2008; dda 21211 [2 CDs]).

12 Concerti Grossi after Geminiani's Sonatas for Violin and Basso Continuo Opus 1, The Avison Ensemble, directed by Pavlo Beznosiuk (Divine Art, 2007; dda 21210 [2 CDs]).

Pieces in collections

Concerto Opus 9, No 11 in A on *A second Recital by the Academy of St Martin in the Fields*, directed by Neville Marriner (L'Oiseau-Lyre (Decca), 1963, SOL 264 [LP only]).

Concerto No 13 in D major (from *Twenty Six Concertos*) on *Music in London 1670-1770*, The English Chamber Orchestra, directed by Emanuel Hurwitz (Decca Eclipse, 1966; ECS 741 [LP only]).

Christmas Hymn (Glory be to God on high) on *The Sounds of St Nicholas*, Choir of the Cathedral Church of Newcastle upon Tyne, directed by Russell A Missin (Mawson and Wareham (Music) Ltd., Newcastle upon Tyne, 1980; MWM 1025 [LP only]).

Sonata Opus 5 No 2 in C minor for harpsichord, two violins and cello on *A Golden Treasury of Georgian Music*, London Baroque, leader John Toll (Saydisc Records, 1984; CD-SAR 66).

Sonata Opus 5, No 2 in C minor for harpsichord, two violins and cello, on *English Music of the 18th Century*, London Baroque, leader John Toll (Amon Ra Records, 1984; CD-SAR 14).

Sonata in F major, transcribed from the original (for violin and keyboard) by R Atkinson, on *English Music for Bassoon and Piano* (ASV, 1985; CD DCA 535).

Concerto No 9, from 12 concertos after D. Scarlatti, English Concert Orchestra, directed by Trevor Pinnock (Arch, 1986; 415 518-1AH [LP only]).

Concerto Opus 9, No 2 in D major, transcribed for organ by Ian Brunt (Hadrian Records, 1991; HDN 911 [cassette tape only]).

Concerto Opus 9, No 3 in A major, Concerto Opus 9, No 6 in E minor, transcribed for organ by Ian Brunt on The Avison Legacy (Hadrian Records, 1992; HON 922 [cassette tape only]).

Concerto No 1 in A after Domenico Scarlatti, from "The Grand Tour": live recording 15th Anniversary Concert; the Avison Ensemble, directed by Timothy Roberts (Avison Ensemble, 2000, SC285-2)

Concerto Grosso Opus 3, No 2 in E minor, No 6 in E major, Concerti after Scarlatti No 12 in D major on *Concertos from the North*, The Avison Ensemble, directed by Pavlo Beznosiuk (Cavalier Classics, 2003).

Select bibliography

Avison, Charles, *An Essay on Musical Expression* (London: C. Davies, 1752).

Avison, Charles, *An Essay on Musical Expression*, 2nd edition (London: C. Davies, 1753).

Baillie, John, *An Impartial History of Newcastle* (Newcastle, 1801).

Bourne, Henry, *The History of Newcastle upon Tyne or the Ancient and Present State of that Town* (Newcastle upon Tyne: John White, 1736).

Burchell, Jenny, *Polite or Commercial Concerts? Concert Management and Orchestral Repertoire in Edinburgh, Bath, Oxford, Manchester, and Newcastle, 1730-1799* (New York and London: Garland Publishing, 1996).

Corp, Edward T., 'Further Light on the Career of "Captain" François de Prendcourt', *Music and Letters*, lxxviii (1997), 15-23.

Cowper, Spencer, *Letters of Spencer Cowper, Dean of Durham, 1746-1774*, ed. Edward Hughes, Surtees Society 165 (Durham/London: Andrew and Co./Bernard Quaritch, 1950).

Cudworth, Charles, 'Avison of Newcastle, 1709-1770', *Musical Times*, cxi (1970), 480-3.

Defoe, Daniel, *A Tour thro' the Whole island of Great Britain* (1724-6) (London: Frank Cass, 1968).

Dubois, Pierre (ed.), *Charles Avison's Essay on Musical Expression, with related Writings by William Hayes and Charles Avison* (London: Ashgate, 2004).

Edwards, Owain, 'Charles Avison, English Concerto-Writer Extraordinary' *Music Quarterly*, lv (1974), 5-23.

Fiennes, Celia, *The Journeys of Celia Fiennes* (1698), ed. Christopher Morris (London: Cresset Press, 1947).

Hawkins, Sir John, A *General History of the Science and Practice of Music* (London, 1776) (New York: Dover, 1963).

Horsley, P. M., 'Charles Avison: The Man and his Milieu', *Music and Letters*, lv (1974), 5-23.

Arthur Hutchings, *The Baroque Concerto* (London: Faber, 1973).

Janssons, Uta, *Matthieu Maty and the Journal Britannique, 1750-1755: a French View of English Literature in the middle of the Eighteenth Century* (Amsterdam: Holland University Press, 1975).

Kingdon-Ward, M., 'Charles Avison', *Musical Times*, xcii (1951), 398-401.

Lubbock, Constance A., *The Herschel Chronicle: The Life-Story of William Herschel and his Sister Caroline Herschel* (Cambridge: Cambridge University Press, 1933).

Mackenzie, E., *A Descriptive and Historical Account of the Town and County of Newcastle upon Tyne, including the Borough of Gateshead* (Newcastle: Mackenzie and Dent, 1827).

McVeigh, Simon, *Concert Life in London from Mozart to Haydn* (Cambridge: Cambridge University Press, 1993).

McVeigh, Simon, 'Felice Giardini: A Violinist in late eighteenth-century London', *Music and Letters*, lxiv (1983), 162-172.

Milner, Arthur, 'Charles Avison', *Musical Times*, xcv (1954), 16-18, 73-5.

Roberts, William, *A Dawn of Imaginative Feeling* (Carlisle: Northern Academic Press, 1996).

Sadie, Stanley, 'Garth, John' Grove Music Online, http://www.grovemusic.com (Accessed June 19, 2008).

Southey, Rosemary, *Commercial music-making in 18th century North-East England: a pale reflection of London?* (PhD Dissertation, University of Newcastle upon Tyne, 2001).

Southey, Roz, 'Competition and Collaboration: Concert Promotion in Newcastle and Durham, 1752-1772' in *Concert Life in Eighteenth-Century Britain* ed. Susan Wollenberg and Simon McVeigh (London: Ashgate, 2004), 55-70.

Southey, Roz, *Music-making in North-East England during the 18th Century* (Ashgate: London, 2006).

Southey, Roz, 'The Role of Gentlemen Amateurs in Subscription Concerts in North-East England during the eighteenth century' in *Music in the British Provinces, 1690-1914* ed. Rachel Cowgill and Peter Holman (London: Ashgate, 2007), 115-128.

Stephens, Norris Lynn, *Charles Avison, An Eighteenth Century English Composer, Musician and Writer* (University of Pittsburgh, PhD Dissertation, 1968).

Weber, William, *The Rise of Musical Classics in Eighteenth-Century England: a study in canon, ritual and ideology* (Oxford: Clarendon Press, 1992).

Welford, Richard, *Men of Mark 'Twixt Tyne and Tweed* (London: Walter Scott, 1895), 55-160.

Wilkes, Lyall, 'Charles Avison', *Journal of the British Music Society*, 9 (1987), 1-6.

The Subscribers

A

Marion Anderson of Gosforth

Rodney Atkinson of Stocksfield

Richard Avison of London

B

Diane Bailey-Ginever of Rochdale

Frances Benton of Sommant, France

Sheila Best of Newcastle upon Tyne

John Birks of Loddefjord, Norway

Mark Stewart Boge of Queensland,
Australia

Tim Bolton-Maggs of Edinburgh

Mr J C & Mrs V E Braithwaite of
Ponteland

Patricia T Brodie of Ryhope Village

Olive & Duncan Brodie of Morpeth

Geoffrey Brown of Barton Upon Humber

M & A Browning of Berkhampstead

Dr Lawrence G Bryson of Gateshead

C

Mr Chris Calver of Newcastle upon Tyne

George Carlaw of Sommant, France

Jane Carroll of Gosforth

Peter & Dilys Carter of Alnwick

Dorothy P Childs of Cramlington

Paul Clarke of Norwich

Mr Robert Arthur Colley of Portsmouth

Linda Collier of Brighton

Mrs Mary Conn of Newcastle upon Tyne

Elizabeth Conran of Barnard Castle

Arnold J Cooper of London

Cynthia Cordery of West Bridgford

Howard Craggill of Twyford

Griselda and David Cuthbert of Hexham

D

Stephen Daglish of Burnham

Michael N Davidson of Southwell

Stanley N Davidson of Newcastle upon
Tyne

W G Day of Winchester

Susan Dean of Stanley

Eileen Dee of Brighton

Carol Dent of Cheadle

Mr Gordon Dixon of Newcastle upon
Tyne

Brian Dotson of Llandrindod Wells

Mrs Mary Dowse of Newcastle upon
Tyne

Anne & James Dowson of Newcastle
upon Tyne

E

Peter Elsdon of Marton-in-Cleveland

Dr Chris Emmett of South Shields

F

Leo Finn of Edenhall

Alice Finn of Edenhall

Simon D I Fleming, organist of Durham

Hilary Forster of Gateshead

G

Dr Andrew Gant of Oxford

Matthew Gardner of Heidelberg, Germany

Evelyn Gardner of Whickham

Dr D K Girling of Newcastle upon Tyne

Christopher Goulding of Heaton

D W S Gray of Newcastle upon Tyne

Anthea Fraser Gupta of Leeds

H

Mrs Rosemary Hall of Newcastle upon Tyne

Stella Hall of Newcastle upon Tyne

Geoff Harrison of Jesmond

John & Anne Havis of Gosforth

Natsue Hayward of Norwich

Hugh & Jean Hedley of Gateshead

Alex & Maureen Henderson of Stockton-on-Tees

Philip Hobbs of Glasgow

Brian W Hughes of Henley-on-Thames

Caroline J Hughes of Aberdeen

Simon D Hughes of Aberdeen

David Hughes of Whickham

Rev. Terry Hurst of Consett

J

Joan Jackson of Newcastle upon Tyne

Mr Stuart Jennings of Murton

Philip Johnson of Clifton

Norman Johnson of Blaydon on Tyne

Lisa Johnson of Jordanhill

Dr H Diack Johnstone of Oxford

K

David King G R S M of Fareham

L

Henrike Lähnemann of Newcastle upon Tyne

Peter & Pauline Leggott of Jesmond

Dr Herbert Loebl OBE of Newcastle upon Tyne

Mr & Mrs John Lumsden of Ponteland

M

Dorothy Mallory of Edinburgh

Danielle Marsilly of Marcilly Sur Eure, France

E C McGovern of Newcastle upon Tyne

Professor Stephen McHanwell of Kenton

Vincent & Ruth Megaw of Adelaide, South Australia

Father V Melia of Ponteland

Mr & Mrs G C Mills of Berwick-upon-Tweed

Mrs C A Mills of South Shields

Stuart Morland of Whitley Bay

Peter Morris of Newcastle upon Tyne

N

Simon Neal of Wolvercote

Roger Norris of Durham

O

Mrs Patricia A M Oley of South Shields

Peter & Irene Oliver of Ashbrooke

P

Miriam Parker of Hexham

Sue Parker-Madani of Chester-le-Street

Joseph William Pegg of Poole

Mr L Rose & Ms J Pigney of Berwick-upon-Tweed

Mrs Ann Plant of Newcastle upon Tyne

Georgina Plowright of Hexham

Denis E B Pollard of Cardiff

David Procházka of Ohio, USA

Chris Pursar of Sowerby

John Purves of Gateshead

R

Kevin Redgrave of Alnwick

Tom Render of Heaton

Ann & Ray Richardson of Brittany, France

Christine & Layton Ring of Low Warden

Monica Roberts of Cullercoats

Dr D & Mrs L Robson of Gosforth

Enid Rogers of Houghton-le-Spring

Lorna Rozner of Newcastle upon Tyne

The late Ramsey W Rutherford of Durham

S

Sotaro Sato of Shizuoka City, Japan

José Saunders of Belford

Mr Gordon Scott of Jarrow on Tyne

Mark & Jill Scrimshaw of Fenham

Nigel Sherlock of Gosforth

John & Margaret Shipley of Gosforth

Professor David Shuker of Rothley

Esmée Slattery of Gosforth

Jane Slocombe of Norwich

F R & A M Smart of Newcastle upon Tyne

Peter Smith of Ryton

Graham Snowdon of Ponteland

Christopher Southey of Durham

Ron & Joan Southey of Kent

Mark Robinson & Sally Standart of Stocksfield

Dr Norris L Stephens of Pennsylvania, USA

Brian & Felicity Stimpson of Gosforth

Winifred Stokes of North Shields

James Sutton of Wimbledon

Professor John & Mrs Jade Swain of Jesmond

T

Marion Talbot of Pershore

Audrey Taylor of Wallsend

The Bewick Society of Newcastle upon Tyne

The Friends of The Avison Ensemble

The Laurence Sterne Trust of Coxwold

The Natural History Society of Northumbria

The Parish Church of St Andrew, Newcastle upon Tyne

Philip R G Thirkell of Newcastle upon Tyne

Julia Thomas of Glasgow

Fynn Titford-Mock of Newcastle upon Tyne

John Treherne OBE of Whitley Bay

Joan Trinder of Jesmond

Lance Tufnell of Huddersfield

V

John Vernon of Eastbourne

W

Sir Humphry Wakefield Bt of Chillingham

Arthur Wallace of Cramlington

David Walter of Newcastle upon Tyne

Dr Robert Walter Wassell of Hexham

Irene Waters of Bedlington

Dr Laurence Watson of West Rainton

Elizabeth Wei of Cambridge

Roy C Williams of Walthamstow Village

Carole & Ged Wilson of Yarm

Susan Wilton of Wooler

Bill & Moira Wooldridge of Prudhoe

Howard John Wootton of Blanchland

Kay Worswick of Gosforth

Y

Addy Yorath of Thirsk

And numerous anonymous subscribers

Index (nos in bold refer to colour section pages)

Tyne Bridge Publishing is part of Newcastle Libraries.

We publish books aimed at everybody with an interest in Tyneside, its people, places and history. Our titles cover many topics from shipbuilding to architecture, and include biographies of many famous Tynesiders from Thomas Bewick to George Stephenson.

Find us on the internet at www.tynebridgepublishing.co.uk, or send for our free catalogue by writing to Tyne Bridge Publishing, Newcastle Libraries, PO Box 88, Newcastle upon Tyne NE99 1DX.

~

The Avison Ensemble was formed in 1984 by Newcastle-born cellist and musical director Gordon Dixon. He was determined to bring the work of Charles Avison to a wider audience.

2009 celebrates the 300th anniversary of Charles Avison's birth, and the Avison Ensemble has now recorded all of his published works. The Ensemble has also built up a well-deserved reputation as one of the finest period instrument ensembles in the country.

'... they must surely be one of the finest period ensembles now in existence.' (*Early Music Review, 2007*)

To find out more about the Avison Ensemble visit www.avisonensemble.com.